ENIGMA U-BOATS

Breaking the Code

Jak P. Mallmann Showell

Naval
Institute
Press

Above: A convoy heading into a grey cloud bank.

Front cover: U995, now a technical museum at Laboe (Kiel), showing the conning tower during the early 1970s shortly after having been set up on land.

Back cover (clockwise from top right): Naval radio operator; *U564* docking in a U-boat bunker; the mansion of Bletchley Park; reconstructed radio intercept station at Bletchley Park and *U559* which was captured in the Mediterranean. Material taken from U559 enabled Bletchley Park to break into 'Shark', the new four-wheel Enigma code.

Title page: A Type VII with an early conning tower design rolling in what looks like relatively mild seas. This shows how uncomfortable life on board must have been. A boarding party, coming along side in a small boat, would have had considerable difficulties getting on board and risked being washed off the deck before gaining access to the conning tower.

© Jak P. Mallmann Showell 2000

The right of Jak P. Mallmann Showell to be identified as the author of this work has been asserted by him in accordance with the Copyright, Designs and Patents Act 1988.

First published in the United Kingdom in 2000 by Ian Allan Publishing an imprint of Ian Allan Publishing Ltd, Terminal House, Shepperton, Surrey TW17 8AS.

Published and distributed in the United States of America by the Naval Institute Press, 291 Wood Road, Annapolis, Maryland 21402-5034.

Library of Congress Catalog Card Number 00-104257.

ISBN 1-55750-202-1

This edition is authorized for sale only in the United States and its territories and possessions.

Printed by Ian Allan Printing Ltd, Riverdene Business Park, Hersham, Surrey KT12 4RG.

Contents

Acknowledgements

Much of this book is based on documents from U-Boot-Archiv, the International Submarine Archive in Germany. I should like to thank Horst Bredow for guiding me through his extensive collection and Mrs Annemarie Bredow for making my visits so comfortable.

In addition to this major source, I have used notes from the following: KptzS aD (*ausser Dienst* [retired]) Ajax Bleichrodt, 'Professor' Gus Britton, Mike Cooper, Hans-Wilhelm von Dresky, Ralph Erskine, Captain Otto Giese, Konteradmiral aD Eberhard Godt, Wolfgang Hirschfeld (U-boat radio operator, historian and author), Georg Högel (radio operator of *U30* and *U110*), Dr Joachim Kindler (radio operator of auxiliary cruiser *Michel*), Fritz Köhl, KptzS aD Otto Köhler, David Lees, Siebrand Voss (radio operator of *U377*) and Karl Wahnig (U-boat radio operator).

Sadly a good many of these people are now dead, but I am extremely grateful to having had the privilege of learning from them and they must be thanked for leaving some of their memories to enrich the minds of those who are seeking information about Europe's turbulent past.

I should also like to thank the following for helping with this book: The Bletchley Park Trust, Lew Britton, Mrs G. F. Calcutt, Reg Crang (secretary of HMS *Petard* Association), Jack Fletcher, John Gallehawk (archivist at Bletchley Park), Ron and Joan Jeffery, Carole Paton, Hermann and Elsa Patzke, Professor Eric Rust, Horst Schwenk, Ellen Spark, Roger Suiters and Robin Thornton from Dungeness Power Station.

Photographs

Illustrations have been a problem inasmuch as some captures took place during the hours of darkness and the few photographs of U-boats being boarded have often appeared in print. In view of this, I have searched for a fresh collection, showing similar images to those described in the book. I hope that readers will agree that this provides a refreshing insight for visualising the actions at sea.

Unless otherwise directed the photographs have come from the U-Boot-Archiv, including the Walter Schöppe collection, from the author's collection and from people listed in the acknowledgements.

Below: Much of the German fleet was scrapped after World War 1. As the Imperial Navy was reduced in size, it was also given a new image with the name of Reichsmarine. In 1935, two years after Hitler came to power, this was changed once more to Kriegsmarine. The flags flying on these minesweepers are the old ensigns of the Reichsmarine, indicating that the photograph was taken around the time when Enigma machines went through their first sea trials.

Chapter 1
Enigma — The Impenetrable Puzzle

Shortly after World War 1 and the dissolution of the Imperial German Navy, the newly formed Reichsmarine started looking around for increasingly secure methods of transmitting vital messages and by the time World War 2 started, all of the German armed forces had adopted an electric code-writing machine known as Enigma. By the time the war ended, there were some 40,000 of these coding machines in use, many of them with slightly different modifications and each type with its own specific name. The navy's version, for example, was called *Schlüsselmaschine M* (Coding machine M, where *M* stood for *Marine*). However, they all functioned on the same principle.

The Enigma machine had originally been conceived by Arthur Scherbius for maintaining industrial and banking rather than military secrets. The reason for this was that urgent business messages were normally sent by the public telegraph system, which meant they had to be written on paper and taken to a telegraph office. There they were transmitted in Morse code through wires and at the destination they were written once more on paper for delivery by dispatch riders. This lengthy process, involving considerable input from a large number of individuals, left ample opportunities for unscrupulous competitors to gain access to sensitive confidential information.

Incidentally, there were also a number of different code books and many firms included the names of the ciphers they used on their letterheads. These were not conceived for the purpose of secrecy but to cut down the length of the telegrams because charges were calculated partly according to the number of words. The codes made it possible to write frequently used phrases and sentences with just a few letters.

Arthur Scherbius' Enigma machine had the great advantage over existing coding systems that the internal set-up was so complicated that it was considered impossible for an outsider to make sense of the code, even when he had one of the machines at his disposal. What was more, the ciphering operation was so simple that any clerk or secretary could quickly be taught how to master the technicalities and, in addition to this, Enigma was considerably faster than any other method available at the time. Enigma was thought to be secure because the number of variations of the code it generated were virtually unlimited. It was calculated that every book on earth could be coded differently without the machine settings having to be repeated.

Before the introduction of this machine, it was possible to work out the meaning of many types of codes because words with double letters, the presence of vowels and a number of frequently occurring words all presented a lever for breaking-in. Enigma was more difficult in that it produced a different letter even when the same one was being transmitted several times in succession. This was of special interest to the German Navy because its system demanded that critical letters in abbreviations be repeated three times to assure there was no ambiguity. For example, FdU (Flag Officer for U-boats) was sent as FDUUU so as not to confuse it with FdT (Flag Officer for Torpedo Boats) and *U34* became UUUTHREEFOUR.

It is not necessary to go into the complicated intricacies of the machine in order to appreciate the Enigma story. The important point is that the variations in code were greater than the number of grains of sand on earth and this vast number of possibilities from such a relatively simple machine gave the Germans a deep sense of security. Many influential officials were convinced that the code would remain an impenetrable mystery, even if the enemy had an identical machine at his disposal. It was thought that the only time anyone could gain access to the messages was when they captured a machine set up with the current settings, but these were changed so frequently that possession would quickly become worthless.

Enigma was born at a time when radio started making a profound contribution to warfare. The old static positions of World War 1, where thousands of men faced each other in muddy trenches, were giving way to the concept of *Blitzkrieg*, or Lightning War, where troops and machinery were constantly on the move. Fast, efficient and secure communications were becoming a vital weapon for the new, highly mobile style of fighting. A similar picture was also emerging at sea, meaning that intelligence and radio security were passing beyond the stage of being a convenient luxury to becoming a vital necessity.

Working Enigma under battle conditions was indeed incredibly simple and did not require any complicated mathematics. Once the operator had set up his machine with the settings of the day, all he needed to do was to type the message on the keyboard. Each time he pressed a letter, the coded version would illuminate. The complexity of the workings literally revolved around three wheels, one of which rotated by one position every time a key was pressed. So, if the operator kept pressing the same key, he would always get a different code. This sequence did not stop once the wheel had rotated through all positions of the alphabet because a second wheel would then be moved one place to keep producing more variations. There was also then a third wheel and later

This page: Coal-burning minesweepers in the North Sea at a time when the Enigma machine was making its first appearance.

Above: Korvkpt Erich Topp of *U552* sporting his ship-made Knight's Cross. He was the first person to use the telephone conversation technique in earnest, proving that it was possible to scramble spoken words with an Enigma machine under war conditions.

the navy also introduced a four-wheel version. To make matters even more complicated, the process did not stop with the last wheel because there was a stationary reflector at the end which directed the electrical current back through a different set of wires in the wheels. So, technically each letter passed through one stationary and six movable wiring combinations, all of which could be set up in different ways.

At first the navy started experimenting with an army version of the Enigma machine but naval bureaucracy was not terribly keen on this device. The army required something small and highly portable which could easily be carried in the field. Portability was not an issue in sea warfare since every ship could carry a machine of any sensible size. The navy was more concerned that messages remain secret for long periods and therefore wanted to make the deciphering process more complicated to deter any potential eavesdroppers. This was achieved by having a greater choice of wheels. Numbers 1-3 were shared with the other German armed forces, but additional ones were provided for exclusive naval use. By the time World War 2 started, ships could choose any three wheels from a selection of seven and more were added as the years went on.

The naval leadership took the view that the sharing of an Enigma system with other armed services could pre-

Above: Lookouts aboard *U552* on a calm summer's day, standing high up on the conning tower wall for the slight advantage of being able to see a little bit further than when positioned lower down.

sent more problems than possible liaison was likely to solve because the wider use of the code would make it easier for an outsider to gain an insight. This caution proved to have been wise. The Luftwaffe's main operational code was one of the first to be broken because such an abundance of messages were flashed around, even

Above: Wolfgang Hirschfeld, radio operator of *U109*, who helped to carry out the first experiments with the radio-telephone conversation. Hirschfeld kept a secret diary which has been published to become one of the most valuable books of World War 2.

from one land base to another, where more secure telephone lines could have been used. The navy adopted the principle of shutting down ship's radio rooms whenever they were in port. To make this possible, even some buoys away from quays had telephone and telex connections.

The order in which the wheels were placed in the machine varied and so did the starting positions. On top of this, especially sensitive messages could be made even more secure. In such cases the deciphered words would appear as jumbled text but with a code meaning 'for officer only'. When this happened, the machine had to be readjusted with different settings and the code typed in a second time. This would often produce meaningful words, except when the code 'for commander only' appeared at the beginning. When that happened, the machine was once more readjusted and the jumbled letters typed for a third time. Of course, the radio operator did not have the settings for 'officer only' messages and the commander kept his settings locked in the boat's secure cupboard.

As with many other things, this system had a definite weak point and the naval hierarchy did not take the natural curiosity of bored sailors into account. Frequently the officer would rush off to hand the news to the commander, leaving the machine to be retrieved by the radio operator. The curious could count the number of letters in the message and manually click the wheels back that exact number of positions. This then gave them the starting positions and from then on any low ranking sailor could work out the meaning of the 'officer only' messages. Things were not quite that simple for an outsider, who still needed to know which wheels to insert, their correct order and their starting positions, as well as the configuration of the plug board at the front. This information was printed with water soluble ink on something which resembled a combination of blotting paper and soft loo tissue. Not only did the ink run as soon as it became damp, but the paper started disintegrating as well. This was such a problem for U-boats with seawater splashing down the hatch and condensation dripping down cold metal walls that two sets of books were often carried. One of them was kept in a safe place in case the working copy became illegible. To make matters more difficult, though, it could not be kept in a waterproof container because the whole object was for it to fall apart if the boat sank in shallow water from where the enemy might recover it.

In order to appreciate the operational simplicity and the speed with which the coding machine worked, one can look at the radio-telephone technique. This was tried out for the first time as late as the summer of 1942 by Korvettenkapitän (Korvkpt) Waldemar Seidel (commander of the naval arsenal in Lorient) sitting in the radio room on land and Wolfgang Hirschfeld (radio operator of *U109*) in his boat just a few minutes' walk away. On 25 July, Admiral Karl Dönitz used the method in earnest to 'talk' to Kapitänleutnant (Kptlt) Erich Topp (*U552*) in mid-Atlantic. The boat's position had become known during a prolonged defeat and Dönitz asked what had happened. His question was typed into an Enigma machine and transmitted as soon as the radio operator saw the letter illuminate above the keyboard. Topp then answered the questions in a similar manner. It took 75 minutes to pass the equivalent of 18 typed lines of text but it still proved to be an excellent method of getting immediate and specific news from the front.

Left and below: A working Enigma machine on display at Bletchley Park. The plug board can be seen at the bottom or front. Above it is a typewriter-like keyboard, then three rows of letters which light up when a key is depressed and at the top are the three wheels or rotors.

To make messages even more secure, the German Navy introduced a number of different code settings each with a different name. Some of these, such as the auxiliary cruiser code, were used so infrequently that Britain never gained an insight. Raider *Atlantis* (Kapitän-zur-See [KptzS] Bernhard Rogge), for example, was located because she was ordered also to act as submarine supply ship and therefore switched to the U-boat code. Using different codes meant that some units could not read the messages for others, but this was rarely a problem. However, on one occasion, *U48* (Kptlt Herbert Schultze) was on the verge of setting up the first wolf pack attack of the war when it was realised that the boat had been on a mining operation in shallow waters and therefore did not carry a code for communicating with other boats in the area. By the time the news reached the land-based control room for possible retransmission, the situation had changed sufficiently to be obsolete.

Examples of a Few Common Codes Used During the War

- **Hydra.** For ships in the Baltic, North Sea and coastal waters of occupied countries. Initially also used by operational U-boats further afield.
- **Thetis.** For non-operational U-boats in the North Sea and Baltic, used during training and working-up periods.
- **Special Key 100.** A general code for auxiliary cruisers and supply ships while in foreign waters. Some of these ships also had their own individual codes.
- **Tibet.** For supply ships which had taken refuge in neutral countries at the beginning of the war.
- **Freya.** For reconnaissance units and for transmission between Coastal Group Commands and the Supreme Naval Command in Berlin where there were no direct land-line connections.
- **Sleipner.** For units belonging to the Torpedo Trials Centre in the Baltic.
- **Bertok.** The connection between Berlin and the German naval attaché in Tokyo.
- **Potsdam.** For naval units in the Baltic engaged in the invasion of Russia.
- **Triton.** Introduced on 1 February 1942 for U-boats in the Atlantic and called 'Shark' by Allied codebreakers.
- **Medusa.** Introduced early in 1943 for U-boats in the Mediterranean.
- **South.** A general code for ships and U-boats in the Mediterranean and the Black Sea.
- **Hermes.** For German naval units in the Mediterranean.
- **Neptun.** For large surface warships when at sea for special operations.
- **Aegir.** For surface ships which were expected to be away from Germany for longer periods.

Above: The later, four-wheel Enigma machine, which was adopted by the navy in 1942, with the cover over the wheels hinged up. One of the alternative wheels is lying on the left and a wire for the plug board can be seen towards the right. In the background are two boxes for storing further spare wheels.

Despite all this complexity of codes, the navy inadvertently also introduced a number of weak points and there were fairly frequent occasions when individuals made quite enormous mistakes. For example, before the war at least one operator was severely reprimanded for sending the same message in plain text and in code. Being tired, he crossed out the decoded message and sent the original text. Realising his mistake, he stopped, added his own explanation and then started again with the same message in code, giving any eavesdropper a real feast of an opportunity.

Strangely enough, later during the war, the German Navy actually started doing something similar as a matter of routine, without realising what brilliant opportunity was being offered to the Allied cryptanalysts. Thinking that the main radio codes had possibly been compromised, the navy adopted a new procedure for operational units at sea. At the same time, many training units and other seemingly less important communications lines continued using the old system. Some of these were the Luftwaffe's weather flights, which flew regular sorties into the Arctic seas, reporting meteorological data. Aircraft flew across the Atlantic as far as Greenland, coming down to sea level to determine air pressure, precipitation, cloud cover, direction and force of the wind and so on. Then the aircraft climbed high to take barometric readings at different altitudes before returning again to sea level. Guns were shot into the water, and the speed and direction of the wind estimated from the appearance of the spray. All this information was radioed back to base in a code which the Allies could understand. At regular intervals, the collated data was retransmitted in the more complicated code used by operational units at sea and weather forecasting stations on land. Since the Allies knew the content of these messages this helped them discover the current settings for the Enigma machines and hence enabled them to decipher other operational messages. It was therefore vital that Allied forces should not hunt down these weather flights because otherwise a vital tool for decrypting the enemy code would be lost. Hence German weather flights continued almost under enemy protection.

The main Allied organisation working to decode German signals was the (British) Government Code and Cipher School (GC&CS) located at Bletchley Park. This organisation is referred to by the term Bletchley Park throughout this book. Strictly speaking Bletchley Park was a large and somewhat imposing country house in the small village of Bletchley, now part of Milton Keynes new town, but before the war in deepest isolation in the rolling Buckinghamshire countryside. The area was chosen because many specialists working on the decryption of radio signals were picked from among the academics at the Universities of Cambridge and Oxford, and Bletchley was roughly half-way between the two. The Park itself was selected from the other short-listed properties in that area because the main house was only five minutes' walk from the main line railway station with

Above: A 10-wheel Enigma type of machine on display at Bletchley Park, used originally for communications of the highest order. The box on the right contains a number of relays which automatically changed channels, making it exceedingly difficult to crack its code. Bletchley Park never succeeded in gaining an insight into this machine.

good connections to London and the university towns. In addition to this there was a new telephone repeater station in Bletchley and a large number of recently laid telephone cables running along the railway lines. Having its own water supply and electricity generators was an added attraction because this meant the place was not dependent on the public supplies which might start faltering in time of war.

The original mansion soon grew into a massive empire with a rabbit warren of primitive huts, employing over 12,000 people working in continuous shifts to keep the decryption process running for 24 hours a day. The operation was so confidential that many of the employees did not know what their neighbours were doing and the whole process remained highly secret until the last of the mechanical Enigma-type machines in foreign countries were replaced by faster and more sophisticated systems. Then, slowly, the secret escaped and a number of highly talented people started telling the story of one of the 20th century's most stunning achievements — a truly remarkable and almost unbelievable accomplishment.

These days, more than 50 years after the end of the war, it is impossible to re-create the whole story of how the secret of Enigma was cracked. German records were confiscated immediately after the war and history written according to how the Allies wanted the world to see their actions. Not only did this lead to the suppression of information but also to the creation of false stories. The secrecy around Bletchley Park was, of course, even stricter than for run-of-the-mill military events. Both Britain and America maintained their stance that the German radio codes had been too difficult to penetrate. Throughout the war they showed very little apparent interest in code-

Above: Land-based stations also used this more sophisticated version of the Enigma machine. Despite there being twelve wheels, Bletchley Park succeeded in reading the code it generated. This was incredible and even more astonishing when one realises that the British experts did not see the machine until after the end of the hostilities. This type did not have a keyboard. Instead it read messages from punched paper tape which increased the speed of transmission.

Above: The radio operator of *U552* working his Morse key to transmit messages. Above his head is a switch box with fuses in white ceramic holders. The earphones deserve a special mention because these still contained a mass of wires in electro-magnets, making them very heavy. Wearing them for any prolonged period was considerably more tiring than using their modern counterparts.

attempt was made to capture a second weather ship, this time the trawler *Lauenburg*. This gave Britain the necessary information for Bletchley Park to understand a good volume of the secret U-boat code. Sadly for Britain, a few months later Germany introduced a new system with an additional wheel, causing a sudden blackout at Bletchley Park. This time things were made considerably more difficult; though, fortunately for the Allies, this was not a universal change. It was only the U-boat code which was made more secure by using four thinner wheels to fit into the space earlier occupied by the three standard wheels. The other German armed forces continued mostly using the old, three-wheel system because the majority of Germans still did not agree with the U-boat chief that the code had been compromised.

Weather ships had ceased to exist and there was no point in attempting another capture because small surface vessels did not carry the new, secret, four-wheel Enigma. For a long time it looked as if Bletchley Park was going to remain locked out in the cold. Once again luck played that vital role and in October 1942 men from the Royal Navy succeeded in getting into *U559* to recover the vital parts to allow the cryptanalysts back into Enigma.

breaking, spreading the misconception that Enigma was indeed an impenetrable puzzle. Yet, Bletchley Park achieved the impossible and cracked the code. The strictness of this security can well be illustrated by an event which took place fifty years after Bletchley Park was closed. A husband and wife who had been married since shortly after the war had no idea that they had both worked at Bletchley Park until each separately received an invitation to attend a reunion there.

By early 1941, despite various successes with German codes, Bletchley Park had reached the stage where its cryptanalysts would definitely benefit by obtaining a fully functioning Enigma machine together with the necessary documentation to operate it. To this end, plans were made to capture the necessary material from a German weather ship, the *München*, whose position had become known through radio direction finders. This had hardly been accomplished when the Royal Navy made an unexpected and incredible contribution by capturing a U-boat, *U110*, without the survivors from the crew having been aware that their boat had not sunk immediately. The wreck remained afloat long enough to salvage virtually everything which could be removed from the interior.

Yet, despite several such successful hauls during early 1941, Bletchley Park still needed more, and another

Above: Men aboard *U103* demonstrating that loudspeakers aboard U-boats could be used for a variety of purposes other than the one for which they had been designed.

Left: Karl Dönitz wearing the piston rings for a vice-admiral, indicating that this was taken during the earlier years of the war. In 1935, he became the first U-boat Chief and remained in that position until the end of the war, although he was also promoted to Grand Admiral in January 1943. Dönitz was first known as Führer der Unterseeboote (FdU) or Flag Officer for Submarines. Shortly after the beginning of the war, this title was changed to Befehlshaber der Unterseeboote (BdU) or Commander-in-Chief for U-boats.

Below: Karl Dönitz, the U-boat chief, standing in front of a group officers while visiting the 7th U-boat Flotilla. Admirals wore their greatcoats with open lapels to reveal a cornflower blue lining, while other ranks had their coats buttoned up to the neck, as can be seen in this picture.

Left: Hut 4 at Bletchley Park, which used to accommodate the naval intelligence section and where the captured items from *U110* were taken to be evaluated. A near-miss during a bombing raid on 20 November 1940 almost demolished the building, which is now used as a restaurant and by Bletchley Park Club.

Right: The front entrance of the mansion at Bletchley Park with a camouflaged military vehicle drawing away. During the war, the room with the bay window to the left of the arched doorway was used by the Park's director, Lord Dennison. The grey roof in the background is the famous Hut 4.

Left: A general view of the huts at Bletchley Park, photographed during the military vehicles weekend of 1999. Although frail-looking, the timber is still in reasonable condition more than half a century after having been erected and the remains of the bomb blast protection walls can also be seen. These walls were originally as high as the buildings, making the interiors pretty dim. The grass tennis courts on the left had been allowed to go wild and it was Winston Churchill who personally ordered that they should be restored with tarmac so that the staff could use them for recreation. The fact that two tennis courts had to be shared by over 10,000 people might suggest that there were long queues.

Chapter 2
The German Radio System

Long before World War 1, Britain tightened its grip on the Empire by connecting its far reaches to London by telegraph cables. The Germans had only a few foreign colonies and were more or less forced to use these British communication lines to Africa and the Far East, which meant they were at the mercy of a foreign power, who could control what was sent, how it was transmitted and could determine whether vital information reached its destination or not. This considerable disadvantage gave Germany an added impetus to experiment with wireless communications which were then in their infancy and an exceptionally efficient system had been established by the

Above: The three trades in the German Navy which specialised in communications were: signalmen, radio operators and telex operators. Signalmen used flags and the semaphore system or they flashed Morse code with signal lamps. The trade badge on the left arm showed two signal flags of the type this man is seen holding. Being often positioned on a high and somewhat exposed part of the ship meant that a life-jacket was recommended in case he lost his balance and toppled over into the water. Binoculars were essential because messages were often relayed over such long distances that he could not easily have seen the signalman on the other ship. Behind the man is a searchlight type of signal lamp as used by surface ships.

time World War 1 started. This helped make it possible for the light cruiser *Emden* to conduct a brilliant campaign of merchant raiding because she could communicate with friendly merchant ships still at large in order to acquire supplies and coal for her hungry boilers. Although Germany was defeated in 1918, it was apparent that the field of radio was going to play an increasingly important role in the future and, to that end, the navy put considerable effort into establishing an efficient radio network. This programme had hardly been completed by the start of World War 2, but was fully operational by 1941, when U-boats were venturing further afield.

The principle of the German radio net was quite simple. Transmitters attached to permanent and mobile command centres could reach most of Europe and these were supported by more powerful, permanent radio stations. The biggest of these, Goliath, was situated at Kalbe, about half-way between Berlin and Hanover. It could reach around the world and even be picked up by submerged U-boats in the Caribbean, although at times local weather conditions made reception impossible. The transmitters in U-boats were much weaker, meaning the boats ideally had to surface before broadcasting back home. The cables running from the bows and stern to the top of the conning tower served as radio aerials and doubled as anchorages for attaching safety harnesses when men worked on the upper deck. In rough weather, when water washing over these aerials curtailed their efficiency, or when the boats wished to transmit from a submerged position, they could raise a rod aerial to periscope height.

Messages from land were repeated at regular intervals giving every unit at sea an opportunity of catching up on the latest transmission, even if it did not receive the original broadcast due to some disturbance. The signals were numbered, making it easy to determine whether any had been missed. All incoming messages were written on paper and kept in a radio log, to prevent commanders from having to be disturbed with mundane news at the time of its arrival. This signals book was obviously a prime target for a boarder.

The reception station or radio room in a U-boat was about as large as a toilet in a small, modern house. The compartment was cramped and uncomfortable, often cluttered with heaps of electronic gubbins and any empty space filled with record players and other equipment for entertaining the crew. The operators were trained at special schools, having first been selected through a hearing test to ascertain whether they could distinguish the

Above: A U-boat signalman on a U-boat standing in a special frame, high up on the top of the conning tower.

captors highly interested in the German radios because they were considered to be much superior to anything produced in the United States.

A few months after the end of the war, the area around Goliath became part of the Russian Occupation Zone and then the remaining parts of the radio station, such as the aerials and the masts supporting them, were dismantled and taken to Russia, where they are believed to have been reassembled and used for a long time. It is quite likely that parts of this powerful transmitter are still in use today. The aerials were supported by some 20 masts, 175m and 200m high, and about 50km of cable was strung around the 4sq km site. The volume of traffic can partly be judged from the 20cm diameter telephone cable, containing about 1,000 individually insulated wires. This was of such value that it was dug up after the war to be reused for other purposes. In addition to Goliath, there was a U-boat command bunker named Koralle in Bernau near Berlin which was used by Grand Admiral Dönitz towards the end of the war. Of course, there were also other major transmitters in the main naval bases and the U-boat flag officers had their own communication networks.

Radio rooms aboard submarines and other ships were usually shut down once the vessel arrived in port. At sea

delicate sounds made by the radios of the day. In addition to good ears, they also required nimble fingers for tapping Morse keys. This attribute was so valuable that radio operators were hardly ever asked to participate in rigorous manual activity for fear of injury.

People living close to the major radio installations often had no idea of their function and many tales about naval schools, spy schools or special research centres reverberated around the local villages. Civilians were not even allowed into the complexes on most occasions, so when men stationed there were visited by their families, they had to meet in hotels or boarding houses. Of course, the massive spider's webs of aerials made it difficult to conceal such transmitters from anyone with a faint knowledge of the subject.

Immediately after the war the Goliath site was occupied by United States forces and was used to accommodate some 80,000 German prisoners. It is quite likely that the site was chosen because it was surrounded by what has been described as an impenetrable minefield, but very few people knew that this existed only on paper. The Third Reich had never got around to installing the mines. The Americans immediately rendered the transmitter useless by removing valves and other essential parts. Those U-boats which surrendered in the USA also found their

Above: A signalman aboard *U178* under KptzS Hans Ibbeken making contact with a supply ship in the South Atlantic. The men are wearing standard wet weather gear for use on occasions when it was not rough enough for really heavy waterproofs.

Above: Dietrich Epp, First Watch Officer of *U572*, demonstrating that signalmen were not always required to flash Morse messages. On top of the lamp was a sighting tube so that the beam could be lined up accurately with the target. Epp was killed in the North Atlantic in September 1943 while commanding *U341*. The bobble hat was not a present from granny, but proper naval issue for U-boats.

the radio operator was responsible for receiving, decoding and filing the masses of information which flooded in all day long. It was well known that transmitters could be detected by radio direction finders and therefore the sending of messages was kept to an absolute minimum. Essential reasons for transmissions were: sighting reports; warnings about enemy forces or mine barrages; reports about the general situation in the operations area, such as weather, ship movements and details of any escorts; position reports with details of remaining fuel and torpedoes and any other information requested by the U-boat Command.

It was pointed out in the commander's handbook that most of this information could be sent with the short signal code which considerably reduced the possibility of being detected by radio direction finders. Non-urgent transmissions were to be made at night when the U-boat was less likely to be spotted or when close to convoys with a view to preventing the enemy taking evasive action as a result of locating the U-boat with direction finders. However, the Germans thought that these precautions became less important as the boats travelled further away from coasts. It was thought that they were safe from

direction finders once they were 200km from enemy controlled territory. In fact this was not so and from early in the war the British were able to fit their escort ships with radio direction finding equipment.

In addition to the general naval rules, the U-boat Command provided every boat with detailed instructions on how to run the radio room. These emphasised that the commander, rather than the operator, always remained responsible for the radio and he was required to make sure that thoroughness was placed higher on the list of priorities than speed.

The following procedure was adopted to prevent any misunderstandings:

1. The commander would give an oral instruction to send a radio message and specify whether this should go as short or regular signal.

2. The Obersteuermann (Navigator, who also acted as third watch officer, but was a non-commissioned officer in the majority of boats) or the petty officer on duty by the navigation desk wrote the message on to a signal pad kept by the side of the chart. He also added the time and the boat's position, but took care not to write on the lower part of the sheet so that there was room for adding the coded version of the message.

3. The radio operator prepared the Enigma code writer, making sure that it was set up with the correct settings of the day.

4. On receipt of the written message, the radio operator added any other non-important information which might have been waiting for a suitable transmission time.

5. Once this had been done, the radio operator checked the position by comparing the words on his sheet with the chart and he also double-checked any codes extracted by the Obersteuermann from the short signal book.

6. At this stage the whole message was read out to the commander, who would then make modifications or give the order to transmit the signal.

Operational U-boats in the Atlantic were under the direct control of the U-boat Command using this radio system. The Commander-in-Chief for U-boats, Admiral Karl Dönitz, was promoted to Commander-in-Chief of the Navy in January 1943 and his second in command, Kapitän-zur-See and later Konteradmiral Eberhard Godt then took a greater role when his boss was absent on other matters. These two men were backed up by a number of ex-U-boat commanders and a few other specialists.

U-boat flotillas, of which there were a good number, and U-boat flag officers who were responsible for various areas

Above: Men on the top of the conning tower of *U569*. The attack periscope can be seen sticking up out of its support. The spiralling wires were supposed to reduce the wash when water swirled around the raised head. Below it, at the bottom, is the signal lamp, ready for action. The fact that this is lying in its holder would suggest that the boat is near port or some vessel is close by. The man on the left with the binoculars is leaning on the top of a ventilation shaft leading down to the diesel engine room.

Below. Despite modern communications such as two way radios and portable telephones, the modern navy still uses this old and well-tried technique of communicating at sea. Two boats have come close together so that commanders can shout at each other through megaphones. There was nothing at all sophisticated with these. They were made from a cone-shaped tin trumpet with an opening for the mouth or ear at the narrow end. The wires running from the top of the conning tower to the bows and stern served as radio aerials and as anchorage for safety harnesses for men working on the upper exposed deck. The attack periscope, with a small head lens, can be seen slightly raised on the left.

only exercised operational control of U-boats in their immediate coastal waters. These officers were mainly in charge of the organisational side of U-boat life. They looked after the welfare of men in port and supplied boats with stores and saw that maintenance work was put in hand. In addition to this, they provided the other services required to make operations at sea possible. The FdU West (KptzS Hans Rösing), for example, also maintained the massive long wave radio transmitter Basselande, near Angers in France, which was responsible for actually transmitting and receiving the messages for the U-boat Command. The U-boat Operations Room had its own small radio transmitter, mounted on the back of a medium sized lorry, but for most of the time sent messages to the radio station by telex and other land-line communications. The lorry-based radio transmitter was considered important because it made the Operations Room highly mobile and fully independent of any single radio station. Should the nearest transmitter be damaged by an enemy raid, the U-boat Command could instantly have switched to another line of communication.

Left: ObltzS Friedrich Altmeier of *U1227* with his 'whisper bag' or megaphone at hand for shouting instruction to the crew working on the upper deck for docking.

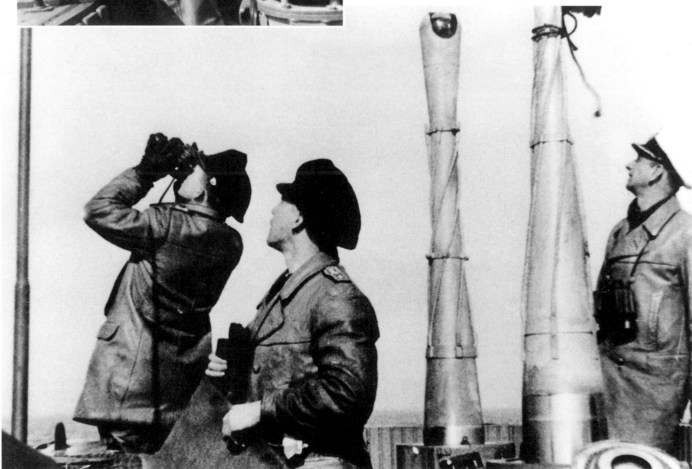

Above: U163, a Type IXC under Kurt-Eduard Engelmann, with both periscopes partly raised. The attack periscope on the right is acting as flagpole. The large head lens of the sky or navigation periscope is clearly visible on the left. The thin rod towards the left of the picture is an extendable rod aerial which could be raised as high as the periscopes. There is a sighting compass at the base of the attack periscope.

Above: A telex operator with his trade badge clearly visible. The chevron below it indicates his rank of Matrosengefreiter or Able Seaman. The man is wearing white denim overalls on top of his blue naval uniform.

Above: This radio tower is made up of three different sets. At the bottom is the basic unit which was fitted to merchant ships and surface raiders. Above it is a U-boat radio and on the top is a receiver for commercial broadcasts.

Above: Telex played a major role in the transmission of information between land-based units of the German Navy. Radio was hardly ever used by ships once they were in port so as to cut down the volume of traffic which might be intercepted by unauthorised ears.

Above: A type of radio for picking up commercial radio stations as used aboard U-boats. It is standing on the top of a cupboard in the U-boat Archive. Behind it is the Maltese Cross of the command flag for an admiral.

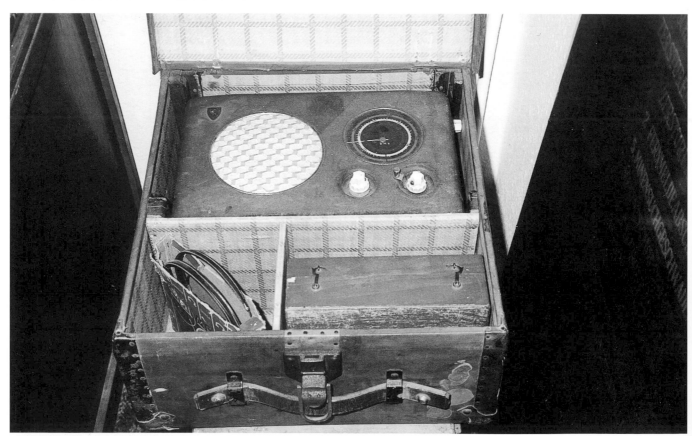

Above: Another U-boat radio in the U-boat Archive, this time inside its strong storage box. These boxes were necessary because boats were often emptied in port and the portable equipment deposited in the flotilla's warehouse. This made cleaning easier and prevented too many people from having access to sensitive equipment.

Above: Photographs of radio rooms in U-boats are exceedingly rare, probably because the space was so confined that there was not enough room to use a standard type of camera. It was also pretty dark and flashbulbs were still comparatively unusual in those days. This previously published photograph shows the radio operators of *U978*. They could cut themselves off from the noise in the boat by closing the door of their tiny compartment. The circular hatch of the bulkhead separating this area from the central control room is just visible on the right.

Above right: The radio operators of *U978* under Günter Pulst. Top left is a loudspeaker, below it a box with fuses in circular ceramic holders and towards the right is one of the main radios.

Right: Funkobergefreiter (Leading Seaman) Schreiber in action with his Morse key.

Right: Funkmaat (Radio Petty Officer) Martin Beisheim of *U758* sitting by his radios.

Below: The radio aboard U-Bauer, a Type XXI now on display at the Maritime Museum in Wilhelmshaven.

Right: Funkmaat (Radio Petty Officer) Steinweg of *U552* using the underwater sound detector. Many commanders were so scared of being detected by Allied direction finders that they shut down their radio rooms at sea and used only the receivers for collecting essential news. In any case, reception was somewhat limited when submerged and it was also the radio team's duty to man this sensitive sound detection apparatus. The hydrophones or underwater microphones were inside a tube-like structure which could be rotated by turning the hand-wheel. The direction of the noise was indicated by a pointer on the dial in the middle.

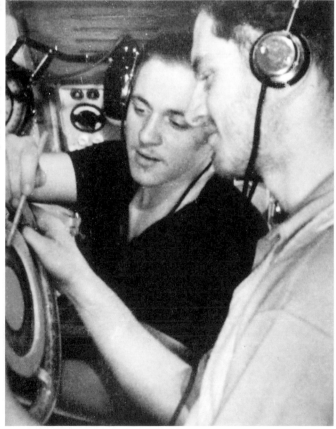

Above: Although relatively simple, finding the direction from which sounds were coming was no easy matter and required considerable practice to get right. The earphones helped by cutting out the bustle from the surroundings, but the boat's own noise from waves bashing against the hull or from running engines made this equipment virtually useless when cruising on the surface.

Above: Fritz-Julius Lemp, commander of *U110*, standing in front of a mobile radio transmitter. Military vehicles had their registration numbers prefixed with WM, WH or WL meaning Wehrmacht (Armed Forces) Marine (Navy), Heer (Army) or Luftwaffe (Air Force). This would suggest that the vehicle is part of a civilian outside broadcasting unit, but mobile military transmitters were similar. A good sized aerial was required and the rack for holding such poles can be seen on the roof, above Lemp's white cap.

Above: The main gate of Château les Pignerolles near Angers, home of the Flag Officer for U-boats: West, who was responsible for organising the facilities in France for Atlantic U-boats.

Above: The grand château was not large enough to accommodate the vast staff required by FdU West and most people worked in huts similar to those at Bletchley Park in England.

Above: The inside of a hut at FdU West. This could really have been anywhere on the Continent. It is only the picture on the wall which gives any indication that it is German. Replace this with a picture of the British king and it could just as well have been at Bletchley.

Above: Radio transmitters require a constant supply of electricity, which was quite a problem in time of war when there were frequent interruptions. This shows an emergency generator at the FdU West complex in France. Bletchley Park had a similar set up, but there it was rarely used until after the war, when a general shortage meant that the machine was set running to keep the heating system functioning on exceptionally cold days.

Above: The power hall for the radio transmitters Basselande near Angers in France from which many U-boat signals were sent into the Atlantic. Not only did these transmitters need a great deal of power, but they also required different types of electricity.

Above: The back of the power hall with radio transmitters behind the men, and replacement parts in the foreground. Note the highly alert guard dog in the foreground.

Above: A close-up of the long wave transmitter Basselande in France from where messages were sent to U-boats.

Above: The control panels for part of the radio transmitters at FdU West in France.

Left: Much of the equipment was duplicated to lessen the chance of mechanical breakdowns, sabotage or air raids putting the system out of action. In addition to this, there were a number of transmitters for different wavelengths. This shows some of the smaller radios at FdU West.

Right: Radio receivers at FdU West in France. Teams of operators constantly monitored a variety of different wavelengths. Yet, despite such intense cover, there were often times when it took several hours before messages from U-boats were acknowledged and at times transmissions were not picked up at all.

Left: Another view of the radio receiving room at FdU West, where U-boat messages were received for the U-boat Command's Operations Room. These operators had no idea what the messages meant, who sent them or their final destination. For them the signals consisted of strings of meaningless letters transmitted in groups of five.

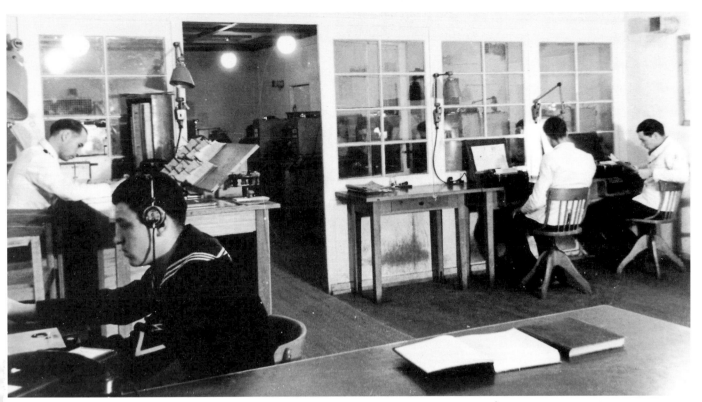

Above: Having received the radio signals, the messages were passed on by dispatch rider, telephone or telex. For this there were 'secret' or 'non-secret' lines, although an unauthorised eavesdropper would not have been able to understand many of the 'non-secret' messages because they were usually still in code.

Above: These are telex machines. The film-reel type of wheel above the desk held punched paper tape for feeding into the code-writer on the right-hand table by the window.

Above: The gas mask containers and tin hats on the shelf indicate that this was a German switchboard, but take these away and this could also have been in England. The jack plug boards were the main exchange junctions for connecting telephone, telex and secret writers to the telephone network. Operators would have connected every call manually. It may be interesting to add that even the fringes of London, such as Bromley and Orpington, still had such manual telephone systems until the later 1950s or even early 1960s.

Right: KptzS Hans Rösing, Flag Officer for U-boats, West on the right and Korvkpt Hans Meckel, one of the first U-boat commanders of the Third Reich, on the left. Meckel was appointed to the position of 4th Staff Officer at the U-boat Command, where he specialised in radio and radar.

Above: U995 near the naval memorial at Laboe (Kiel) showing the rear of the conning tower with improved anti-aircraft armament. There are two twin 20mm and one single 37mm guns. The frame on the left is a combination radar and radar detection aerial.

Right: In translation this document reads: '--Secret-- Hearty congratulations for your commissioning Supreme Commander-in-Chief of the Navy and Commander-in-Chief for U-boats'. Note that the Enigma machine did not have Umlauts, whence 'für' has become 'fuer'.

Marinenachrichtendienst

Ltg.-Nr. ....

Nr. MWHu 873

Nr.	Weiter an	Tag	Uhrzeit	Ltg.	durch	Verzögerungsvermerk
Aufgen., den 14/12 194 4						
um 1545 Uhr						
von ... Ltg. ...						
durch ...						

+LT MEUZ 51094 14/12 1030=

31 UUUFL FUER KPTLT OTTO (PAUL- FRIEDRICH)=

--GEHEIM-- ZUR INDIENSTSTELLUNG HERZLICHEN GLUECKWUNSCH=

OE D M UND BDU+

Funkspruch-Ausgang

Eingang Fernschreibraum		Schaltung	Leit-Nr.	Ausgangszeit	Funkspruch Nr.
				•	
Ausgeschrieben	B. U. Offz.	Alle Wellen!		Offen!	
m.:					

An Schröteler!
Ich habe Ihnen am 2.Mai das Ritterkreuz zum Eisernen Kreuz
verliehen.Mit meinen Gedanken bin ich bei Ihnen und Ihrer braven Besatzung.

Ihr Grossadmiral.

Uhrzeitgruppe	1916/10	
J. T. O. d. Wache		
Lfnr.	Schaltung	Ausgangszeit
A11/260	alle	1933
f33/98	Wellen	1934
d 93		nov.
		Abschr. erledigt:

175 Druckerei M OKM 10000 9 43

Right: This message to the Commander of *U1023* translates as: 'To Schröteler! I have awarded you the Knight's Cross of the Iron Cross on 2 May (1945). My thoughts are with you and your brave crew. Your Grand Admiral'. The person transcribing the message made a mistake — the name should be 'Schroeteler'.

Chapter 3
The First Naval Enigma Wheels — The Sinking of *U33*

It is quite likely that the value of the material captured from *U33* in February 1940 was considerably greater than early accounts would lead us to believe. After all, the Royal Navy undertook a highly precarious and incredibly dangerous dive to retrieve secrets from the sunken wreck. So, early fobbing-off reports relating to the low value of the material recovered could well be part of a determined deception plan. On the other hand, it is now known that Polish cryptanalysts had constructed a number of Enigma machines before the war and passed at least one of these to the British. It is therefore likely that Bletchley Park would already have known the wiring patterns of the wheels recovered from *U33*.

The fact that the Enigma wheels from *U33* fell into British hands can largely be attributed to that massive and most significant factor, the restless ocean, which played such a critical role. Both sides were constantly faced with this neutral opponent. The tempestuous sea did not take sides, but for most of the time added an extra challenging dimension to the warfare in its realm. On this occasion men were defeated by the exceptionally powerful cooling effect of the Atlantic swell and by the surge of strong currents. Anyone who has tried swimming in the waters off western Scotland on hot August days will know that the rocky islands there are guarded by the most ferocious currents and by chilling water temperatures. Without going very far, one finds the cold numbing muscles, while a piercing headache from the iciness quickly drives one back on land. Trying to swim there in winter would have been exceedingly difficult and anyone jumping into the cold water might easily lose consciousness within a few minutes. Even if they remained in control of their bodies for a little longer, the struggle to stay alive would have occupied considerably more energy than one would have imagined before making the decision to jump into the unknown. It is quite likely that the majority of men from *U33* were stunned the moment they hit that icy water. It must be remembered that they were tired and had not exercised for some time. Those who were not suffering from extreme hypothermia by the time they were picked up were already dead. Bearing these atrocious conditions in mind, it is not surprising that the Royal Navy found in the pockets of survivors a number of Enigma wheels that should have been discarded.

Above: One of the wheels or rotors from an Enigma machine. The flat, round brass contacts can be seen towards the left. The clips at 'A' and 'Z' could be pressed to rotate the collar with the letters to any one of the 26 positions. It was common practice to distribute these wheels among the men once boats entered enemy-controlled shallow water, the idea being that they should be thrown away if the boat had to be abandoned.

Below: A storage box for Enigma machine rotors on display at Bletchley Park in England. The pins visible on the left side of each wheel were spring loaded and pressed against the flat plates visible in the previous picture.

U33's mining operation in the Firth of Clyde was not the first attempt at approaching close to British harbours. It was the end of a long chain of events which started soon after the beginning of the war. A general shortage of torpedoes encouraged the U-boat Command to use the plentiful supply of torpedo mines during the long dark winter nights of 1939. Mines were a most powerful weapon in that first winter of war because Germany really did have an effective secret weapon in this field. The magnetic mine created havoc by not responding to what were then the normal minesweeping techniques, nor annoying small ships, but breaking the back of the first good sized vessel to pass over the top. Even if nothing important was sunk, mines still created confusion and delay, and their clearing tied up the opposition. The initial fears of approaching close to British harbours soon dissolved, and later even surface ships crossed the North Sea to lay mines within sight of land.

The fateful voyage on which *U33* was sunk was her second mining operation. The boat had also been in southern Irish waters and, earlier still, it had participated in the Spanish Civil War. This meant that both the crew and the commander, Hans-Wilhelm von Dresky, had as much experience as any other at that stage. Von Dresky had joined *U33* a year before the war, after having served for

a year as commander of *U4*, a small 'dugout' of Type IIA. His humanitarian intentions are best illustrated by the manner in which he applied the virtually impossible Prize Ordinance Regulations. Not only did he tow lifeboats from a ship he had sunk closer to the Irish coast, but he also fired his own distress rockets to attract the attention of a passing neutral rescue ship. Postwar historians, who have often tried to demonise German actions by describing attacks as 'aggressive' or 'brutal', have been unable to apply such descriptions to von Dresky. Therefore a number have gone the other way, and portrayed him as having been unfit to command because he was too soft and unable to plan ahead. Much of this information, probably originating during the war from statements made by survivors, must be taken with a large pinch of salt. First, many prisoners took the opportunity of telling their captors the wildest of misleading details and, second, although the material was distributed confidentially within the Royal Navy, it still contained an unexpectedly high proportion of propaganda aimed at throwing the Germans into a bad light.

Below: U33 on 3 August 1936 during the commissioning of *U21*. Although this photograph has been published before, it is of special interest because a sequence of pictures recently discovered in the U-Boot-Archiv has made it possible to identify the two men in the bottom left. On the left is Kapitän-zur-See und Kommodore Karl Dönitz and standing next to him is Otto Hersing, the famous World War 1 U-boat ace who commanded the first *U21*.

Above: U33 was launched on 11 June 1936 at Germania Works in Kiel while *U31* took to the water for the first time on 25 September 1936 at Deschimag AG Weser in Bremen. The following few photographs show exactly how similar they looked. Had it not been for the numbers on the conning towers, it would have been almost impossible to distinguish one from the other.

Above: U33 in Spain during the Civil War. The vertical stripes on the conning tower were black, white and red, the old German colours used to identify the nationality of the boat.

Above: No marks for guessing the identity of this boat.

Von Dresky was certainly no beginner and he should have been well prepared for the task in hand. What was more, he had a run-in, reliable crew. Everything which happened during that last voyage had been well rehearsed under bitter war conditions while facing a determined enemy. On top of this, statistics throw a totally different light on von Dresky's abilities. He was responsible for sinking the creditable total of 12 ships, although six of these were admittedly small fishing boats of less than 300 tons. Disregarding these tiny trawlers, his score still included half a dozen good-sized ships, meaning he ranks among the top 10% of the U-boat commanders with U33 one of the top 150 highest scoring boats. Taking all 12 sunk ships into account, then only 83 other U-boats from the total of 1,171 equalled or bettered that score. With such impressive ratings it is difficult to understand the majority of negative remarks made about von Dresky by postwar historians.

The procedures for mining close to land had been well perfected by the time U33 sailed from Wilhelmshaven on that bitterly cold February morning. Von Dresky would have discussed tactics with other commanders, and everyone on board would have been given enough information to tackle the task in hand. In addition to this, the men in U33 were almost veterans at dealing with the dangers of shallow coastal waters with treacherous currents. The usual trick was to stow the mines inside the boat and pull out any torpedoes from the tubes shortly before the operation. Carrying mines in the tubes from base was a bad idea because that would have prevented the boat from attacking suitable targets en route. On this occasion U33 carried 12 TMB mines as well as six torpedoes. This meant that everything was accommodated inside the pressure hull and there was no need to transfer torpedoes or mines from external storage containers under the outside deck. Such a transfer would have been rather difficult and, at that time of the year, also life-threatening to the men who would have had to work on the outside for a couple of hours while the seas washed around them.

Secret papers aboard would have been cut down to an absolute minimum; boats on mining operations usually did not carry any documentation which might compromise other operations. Therefore they were very much on their own, not even being able to understand the radio code used by boats around them, though they still had the normal Enigma machine on board as well as all the naval wheels to operate it. Von Dresky probably knew that the daunting task of mining the Clyde estuary had been aborted a few weeks earlier by U32 under Hans Jenisch. Nine months later, Jenisch received the Knight's Cross, indicating that he was no also-ran who might have been put off by a little opposition.

Below: U33 (left), *U31* (centre) and *U30* (right).

Historians have suggested that the crew of *U33* knew they were going on an especially dangerous mission because a high ranking Nazi official visited the boat shortly before departure. It is possible that the crew were aware of the dangers ahead, but the rest of the statement must be put down to the usual cheap propaganda. The high ranking person in question was the U-boat Chief, Admiral Karl Dönitz, who frequently saw off departing boats and was usually there to welcome them back. What is more, *U33's* mission was no more dangerous than the 40 or so successful minelaying operations which had already taken place.

On the evening when *U33* was sunk, HMS *Gleaner* (Lieutenant-Commander [Lt-Cdr] H. P. Price) was patrolling the outer reaches of the Clyde estuary, off the Isle of Arran's southern tip. *Gleaner* has also been recorded as 'Cleaner' and as a minesweeper, but had actually been a survey ship before the war before being given the hasty conversion into anti-submarine vessel which resulted in her being reclassified as a sloop. Fitted with Asdic equipment and an armament of 40 depth charges and a good number of small guns, she was well suited to the task of hunting submarines. It was 0250 hours on 12 February 1940 when *Gleaner's* hydrophone operator reported mechanical noises on the starboard bow. The officer of the watch, Sub-Lieutenant E. P. Reade, brought the ship to action stations and had the captain woken up. The source of the noise was still well over a mile away and, on that dark night, this meant that no one could see the cause of the commotion. Increasing speed, *Gleaner* headed towards the possible intruder.

Forty minutes later, *Gleaner's* searchlight was switched on to illuminate some unusual movement of the water, but nothing definite was seen. There was only a patch of whirling water with traces of white wash, although those who had managed to adjust their eyes and were not dazzled by the intensity of light thought they had caught a glimpse of a periscope as it disappeared below the waves. Four depth charges dropped on the spot produced an unusual result. Instead of damaging the intruder, *Gleaner* was thrown into total darkness as the auxiliary machinery failed. Half an hour later, *Gleaner* was back in business for another attack, this time with five depth charges. Half an hour after that, five more were dropped. This was one of those frustrating occasions when the swirling currents of the Clyde estuary played tricks with the Asdic, causing it to respond to differences in water temperature and possibly rocks in the water. Then the last set of detonations made it give up the ghost altogether. The searchlight had been out of action since the first explosion as well, leaving *Gleaner* in a desperate situation. In the unenviable blackness *Gleaner* had to use two small signalling lamps to try to spot the source of the noise.

It was still dark at 0522 hours when *U33* unexpectedly surfaced a mile or so from the sloop. Guns immediately opened fire and half a dozen rounds from the 4in gun narrowly missed the conning tower. Bringing the engines back to full speed, *Gleaner* tried to ram, but it looked as if the men on the U-boat were surrendering. Swarming over the upper deck they were shouting and waving their arms over their heads. It certainly did not look as if they were about to engage the sloop, so Price swung the helm over and brought his ship to a halt close to the surfaced U-boat. By this time it was obvious that the Germans were calling for help and it looked as if a capture might come off, but this thought was quickly frustrated by an impressive shower of sparks shooting up high from the conning tower. Almost immediately *U33* plunged into the depths. Reports from survivors later confirmed that scuttling charges had been placed under vital secret material, including the Enigma machine, and it could well have been that these detonated too soon.

Gleaner was still experiencing mechanical problems caused by the damage to her own machinery from the depth charge explosions, but Price was intent on saving as many lives as possible and ordered his boats to be lowered to rescue the Germans. Unfortunately the boat crews also found the waters of the Clyde estuary to be exceptionally challenging and at times could hardly make headway against the currents. The trawlers *Floradora* and *Bohemian Girl* also arrived and rescued three officers and seven ratings between them, although a number of these died before the boats reached shore. The *Javelin* Class destroyer *Kingston* arrived later to pick up 22 men of whom only two were still alive. The final count was that 17 men had survived from a total of 42.

Some days later, the minesweeper HMS *Tedworth* arrived at the sinking spot with a group of naval divers to survey the wreck. Since it was known to be lying in deep water, among precarious rocks, dangerous currents and low temperatures this effort would suggest that the Royal Navy was interested in something more specific than just taking a look at the wreck. It seems highly likely that they were after the Enigma machine. Incidentally, one of these divers was Frank William Britton, brother of 'Professor' Gus Britton, Assistant Director of the Royal Navy's submarine museum at HMS *Dolphin* and famous historian, who died recently.

Right: The long, narrow foredeck of *U31* during the Spanish Civil War with the black, white and red vertical stripes on the conning tower. The hole at the front at the base of the net cutter was an outlet for a towing rope. Each boat carried a length of steel cable in a locker situated between the upper deck casing and the pressure hull. However, when the Royal Navy wanted to use this facility for towing *U110* the men found the cable had rusted sufficiently for it to be no longer suitable for the task. The flag in the foreground is of interest. It is the National and Mercantile Flag, usually flown on Kriegsmarine ships before they were commissioned.

Inset: The Kriegsmarine Ensign 1935–45.

Right: U31 battling its way through a brisk sea on a bright day.

Below: U31's rescue buoy floating in the fierce currents of the Jade Estuary in the Schillig Roads after the boat had sunk in March 1940, killing the entire crew.

Above: The foredeck of *U31*. The capstan head of the electric winch can be seen in the background, near the front of the boat. The red and white dome-shaped object with a lamp on the top is the emergency rescue buoy. *U31* was one of the few submarines which used this buoy in earnest, on 11 March 1940, when the boat was sunk by an aircraft in the Schillig Roads outside Wilhelmshaven. The boat was raised, only to be sunk a second time off Ireland on 2 November 1940.

Left: Living within the confines of a submarine, where men could hardly move about, was not only a strain on the muscles but also played havoc with the digestive system. Whenever conditions allowed men took advantage of opportunities for physical activity and various games were devised for keeping fit aboard U-boats. This shows *U33* before the war, at a time when fast diving was not yet a matter of life and death, meaning that it was possible to allow a good number of the crew out onto the upper deck.

Right: The upper deck of *U33* also served as parade ground, being the only place on board where the whole crew could assemble, although such formality was a rarity. It was usually only shortly before and after a cruise that the whole crew would be expected to parade en masse.

Above: Adolf Hitler, shaking hands with Kptlt Hans-Wilhelm von Dresky. The photograph is of interest because the 'Kriegsmarine' hat band of the man at the back suggests that this was taken after the beginning of the war on 3 September 1939. However, Karl Dönitz, the U-boat Chief (second from left) is wearing his coat buttoned up to the top which would indicate that this was before he was promoted to Konteradmiral in October 1939.

Left and above: A Type VIIA showing the above-deck torpedo tube aft.

Chapter 4
Weather Ships for Bletchley Park

A costly error by the British high command during the first year of war led to the loss of an aircraft carrier, two destroyers and the lives of 1,515 men. The sad point about this tragedy was that it could have been averted, had the admirals listened to Harry Hinsley, then a young graduate working at Bletchley Park. (Hinsley later wrote the British Official History of Intelligence Operations in World War 2). By analysing the nature of radio signals which could not yet be decrypted, he informed the navy that powerful German forces were on their way north. No one took any notice of this unknown civilian and British ships participating in the evacuation of the Narvik area of Norway were not even warned. Consequently the aircraft carrier *Courageous* (Captain [Capt] D'Oyly-Hughes) and the destroyers *Acasta* (Commander [Cdr] Glasford) and *Ardent* (Lt-Cdr Barker) were surprised by a German squadron, made up of the battlecruisers *Scharnhorst* and *Gneisenau*.

The original story released by the British authorities stated that the two destroyers and the aircraft carrier went down so quickly that none of them had time to transmit a sighting report and therefore so many men ended their days in the cold waters off Norway. However, recently a television programme has suggested that there is evidence of a vital distress call having reached London, but that the only possible rescue ship was the cruiser *Devonshire* with the Norwegian king on board and it was thought unwise for such an important ship to be diverted and delayed. Hinsley said in his official history that he could understand the navy's reluctance to listen to a civilian who was basing his deductions on an untried and not yet understood method of drawing conclusions from the type of signals flowing through the ether. Whatever, this disastrous event made even hardened sceptics at the Admiralty sit up and take notice of the youngsters at Bletchley Park.

Several other incidents during 1940 also drove home the fact that the best raw information is of no use to operational commanders unless they are able to interpret it. Take the first aerial reconnaissance flights over Kiel in North Germany as an example. These photographs, taken in March 1940, showed a busy harbour full of shipping, but no one in Britain knew whether this was normal or not. A few days later, when Germany launched its invasion of Norway and Denmark, the British photographic interpreters realised they had seen the evidence of

Below: A patrol boat or Vorpostenboot similar to *Krebs*, which was boarded by the Royal Navy. These were deep sea trawlers before the war but the massive aerial strung between the masts indicates that this is no ordinary fishing boat. A gun has been added to the bows and a firm lookout platform on the foremast. In 1940, stern trawlers were still an invention of the future and boats like *Krebs* had their machinery and living quarters aft of the wheelhouse while most of the hard fishing work was carried out from the exposed foredeck.

this massive undertaking. But without previous reconnaissance flights, they did not have the means of extracting that vital information from the pictures in front of their eyes.

By the beginning of 1941 the Admiralty in London was more ready to listen to the backroom boys. In fact, the navy even established liaison officers to commute between various centres to ensure there were ample channels for the flow of essential information. One of these men pricked up his ears when Hinsley told him how they could lay their hands on an Enigma machine. Hinsley had been scanning through intercepted messages from German weather ships positioned far out in the Atlantic and had come to the conclusion that they must have Enigma machines on board. The pattern of their radio transmissions suggested the jumbled letters had not been created by a manual cipher pad.

Initially this idea was not even fully accepted by Hinsley himself. It seemed probable, but he could not believe that the Germans would allow such a valuable machine into a highly precarious position. Yet, the more Hinsley examined the meaningless text, the more convinced he became that the code was generated by an Enigma machine and a weather ship offered an excellent opportunity for trying to capture such a priceless device.

Weather forecasting had become a major problem in Germany. The war shut down many weather stations and those which remained were transmitting in code. The basic raw data for meteorological conditions were essential for forecasting the weather over Europe and therefore Germany employed a variety of different tricks such as sending out weather ships, organising weather flights and

later even setting up manned and unmanned weather stations on land and floating at sea. This chain of fascinating events has been very much neglected by historians, but played a significant role throughout the war. Although several authors have suggested that weather details were collected for specific purposes such as directing U-boat wolf packs or for the planned invasion of the United Kingdom, this is not entirely true. The data collected by these observatories were used by the German meteorological offices for general forecasting, and details from the Atlantic and Arctic were important because many of the weather systems moved from west to east.

The weather ships on which Hinsley was concentrating were converted deep sea trawlers sent out for a period of several weeks with the objective of recording and transmitting two daily reports. Most of these ships were manned by prewar fishermen who were supplemented by a number of military specialists to help with those jobs for which the fishermen had not been trained. This included keeping the radios functioning, advising on naval matters and manning the meagre armament, though one wonders why these tiny ships were fitted with armament at all. Much of their shooting power was so weak that the guns were of hardly any use, not even against a single small aircraft.

The snag with Hinsley's suggestion was that the capture of a weather ship could create more problems than it solved. Bletchley Park had made considerable inroads into the German cipher system and disclosing that interest might force the Germans to adopt a different process altogether, thereby totally defeating the object of the exercise. At this point the British were still unaware of the German paranoia about being detected by radio direction finders and thought any aggressive action against these lonely weather ships would force the opposition to conclude that their radio codes were being compromised.

The first capture of a converted trawler, the patrol boat (*Vorpostenboot*) *V2623* on 26 April 1940 while on passage from Germany to northern Norway, had done nothing for the British cryptanalysts. Hinsley has stated that the boarders were more interested in looting than locating radio secrets. The best part of a year passed before another opportunity of boarding a ship came along, but this happened during the early stages of a commando raid on the Lofoten Islands in March 1941 and searching enemy boats was not on the list of priorities. In fact the boarding did not take place until a long time after the patrol boat *Krebs* had been shot into submission by the destroyer *Somali* and left burning. On the way back after the raid, and finding the wreck still afloat, a boarding party recovered enough confidential material for Bletchley Park to read a considerable proportion of the radio traffic throughout March 1941. The fact that this was only achieved towards the end of April and much of the news was no longer of any great operational value did not matter. The experts at Bletchley Park felt elated at having achieved what had been claimed to be impossible — they had cracked the impenetrable puzzle. In addition to this, the acquired material suggested to Hinsley that such small boats carried so much coding material that a future intentional capture might prove highly profitable even if the obvious prizes of the machines themselves and the current settings were destroyed. Incidentally, the name of the patrol boat, *Krebs*, has usually been translated as 'crab' or 'shrimp', neither of which is technically correct. She belonged to a group named after stars and signs of the zodiac and therefore the correct translation should be 'Cancer'.

The material recovered from the *Krebs* contributed towards the Admiralty deciding that the risk of a possible capture not coming off was worth taking, and soon the backroom boffins were joined by operational commanders to sift through information to find the most vulnerable weather ships. It appeared as if there were always two of them at sea. One was positioned in an unfrequented area of the Atlantic to the south of Iceland and the other further north in the Arctic. Intelligence which emerged during March 1941 suggested that these ships carried not only an Enigma machine but also a weather cipher and the short signal book. Interrogation of survivors from U-boats and other German ships suggested that this last code was taking an increasingly great role in the Battle of the Atlantic and finding a copy would be more than useful for Bletchley Park.

Above: Waves frequently washed over the deck of patrol boats, soaking the men who worked there. This was not all that unusual before the war when many people lived, worked and died in unbelievably poor conditions.

Right: The weather ship *Sachsen* in Bordeaux. The boat looks especially clean and tidy because it has just come from a major overhaul and is now getting ready for sea. Something official has got to be going on because otherwise the man would not be wearing such a good uniform. Like the U-boat crews, the men who manned these boats cared little for official regulations and usually wore functional, comfortable clothing rather than correct uniform.

In the end, the navy decided to go for the weather ship positioned to the north of Iceland, but the powerful force of three cruisers, *Birmingham*, *Edinburgh* and *Manchester*, together with four destroyers, *Nestor*, *Bedouin*, *Eskimo* and *Somali*, waited until early May when a new trawler had just taken up position, the reason being that a fresh boat would carry the code settings for the longest period. The passage northwards was relatively easy, although it was not without tension. Obviously very few men knew about the planned capture and those that did were also aware of the Luftwaffe's weather flights. Being sighted by one of these aircraft could quickly frustrate the whole venture. There were a few nerve-tingling, cold days until the 306-ton, coal-burning *München* was sighted. The British force went in immediately. At her top speed of 32 knots the *Somali* bore down on the ill-fated little trawler.

Below: Sailors hardly ever waste anything and left-overs are thoroughly inspected before being discarded. This joint obviously still has sufficient meat left on the bone.

The approaching destroyer was sighted at around 1700 hours on 7 May, just as the latest weather report was being transmitted. This meant that the vital coding tools were lying around the radio room. The British guns had hardly opened up when news of the attack was reported to base and the Enigma machine, together with code books, thrown overboard. Some of the more experienced German sailors even realised what was happening. The roar of the guns and the noise from detonations did not match the usual intensity of destruction, suggesting that the approaching ship was not using normal ammunition. Special lead-weighted bags at hand for such an event were grabbed and filled with everything lying on the table. Tossing these overboard was easy, though one of the bags contained sufficient air not to sink at first.

The boarders from HMS *Somali* found the nest empty of the most significant finds. However, this time the men had been specially trained and immediately went below to search the officers' and the commander's quarters, where they were rewarded with a set of out-of-date papers. These were easily identified because they were usually bound in red covers. When this material arrived at Bletchley Park, cryptanalysts described it as 'unexciting and commonplace', although it did enable the experts there to read the code retrospectively. Sadly for the men who put so much effort into capturing the *München*, they were upstaged a few days later by the secret capture of *U110*. Bletchley Park was having a field day, but despite the massive haul from *U110*, there were still holes in the system and it was decided to have another go at a second weather ship. Less than two months later, the Royal Navy was pitched against the trawler *Lauenburg*, shortly after she had replaced the *Sachsen* on weather patrol duties. Getting at her with superior fire-power was easy. The difficult part was to reach her before the men had time to jettison those vital documents.

This time the attacking force consisted of the cruiser *Niagara* with the destroyers *Bedouin*, *Jupiter* and *Tartar*. Despite having learned lessons from previous attempts, they still were not in time to lay their hands on the Enigma machine, but the boarders did come away with a haul of valuables. Much of this ended up in Hut 8 at Bletchley Park, where every possible advantage was squeezed from it.

Right: An Obermaat or Chief Petty Officer of the weather ship *Sachsen*. His rank is indicated by cornflower blue patches with gold bars on the lapels. The ribbon through the buttonhole indicates that he has been awarded the Iron Cross Second Class. This medal was worn only on the day of issue or with full formal dress. On other occasions only the ribbon was worn as is shown here.

Left: The wheelhouse of the weather ship with the open bridge above it. Directing the ship from the wheelhouse in bad weather would have been difficult because there were no window wipers, meaning visibility was severely restricted. Working on such small ships was a cold and wet occupation for much of the year.

Below: Aboard the weather ship *Sachsen*.

Above: The original caption of this photograph by Walter Schöppe states: '7 June 1941 in Bordeaux. The brave men of the *Sachsen* talking to war correspondents Beilstein and Göbel.'

Above: All the weather ships and many of the patrol boats were hastily converted fishing boats.

Chapter 5
U-boats at Sea

Left: Confidential materials were usually locked away in a safe depository on land once the boat put into port. At the same time, the majority of the crew moved out to be accommodated elsewhere while only a few men remained behind. This shows part of the naval complex in Kiel where U-boat men lived for some of their time in port.

Above: Kiel and many of the other harbours were guarded by a number of defences, making it difficult for seaborne forces to attack U-boats in port. However, experts such as Günther Prien and Otto Kretschmer still took precautions to protect their boats, saying it would be easy for the defences to be penetrated by a determined enemy. This shows the narrow channel approaching Kiel. The old muzzle loading gun battery at Möltenort, on the right, had been converted into a U-boat memorial by the time World War 2 started and the spit of land connecting the Friedrichsort lighthouse to the western shore also made it difficult for ships to approach the Kiel base, which was situated several kilometres further inland. A massive submarine net made access through the narrows even more hazardous.

Top left: Guard duty was one of the most boring and hated occupations in port. At least one man from each crew was usually positioned inside or outside the boat to check who was boarding or going ashore, although these guards were not always armed.

Above: Retractable bollards were used to secure U-boats. Ropes could not be tied just anywhere because the deck casing was relatively flimsy and the boat was heavy enough to pull much of it off. This is *U178*.

Left: Having cast off, a U-boat usually followed an escort out into deep water. Mines dropped from aircraft and by submarines, as well as attacks from the air, had become a serious threat. This shows *U178* nosing her way out into the Bay of Biscay behind a Sperrbrecher or minesweeper.

Right: Once close to port, the majority of the crew could relax and even the lookouts were no longer bound to their sectors. Instead they could peer at whatever took their interest. The pennant indicates that this boat is returning after having sunk a ship of an estimated 4,000 tons. The attack periscope is raised, probably to hold up the flags. The grids over the ventilation shafts can be seen on both sides.

Below: At sea, lookouts operated under considerably stricter rules. Each man had his own overlapping sector and was forbidden to turn his attention to other areas, even when there was something terribly exciting going on behind his back. This shows *U181* under Wolfgang Lüth, who can be seen on the bottom right. He was one of only two U-boat men to have been awarded the Knight's Cross with Oakleaves, Swords and Diamonds. The periscope support with sighting compass can be seen in the middle.

Right: Days when lookouts had easy, leisurely options were comparatively rare. For most of the time U-boats operated in severe conditions where a four-hour-long spell on the top of the conning tower was quite a punishment. This shows men from *U760* under Kptlt Otto-Ulrich Blum with the barrel of a 20mm anti-aircraft gun on the right.

Bottom: Seeing the enemy before being spotted was an essential part of the survival process and lookouts falling asleep were severely punished. Constantly sweeping glasses over an empty horizon was a soul-destroying but necessary occupation. Royal Navy research showed that a submarine lookout would spend the best part of 30 minutes cleaning his glasses during each four-hour-long duty spell.

Left: Life jackets were carried by some boats, but many saved space by using submarine escape apparatus instead which doubled up as flotation aid. The two men on the right from *U195* are wearing Dräger Lungs in this way.

Below: A Dräger Lung in use inside the diving tank at the submarine school.

Above: A man from *U178* wearing a Dräger Lung, named after the firm which made it. Ironically, the same firm made breathing apparatus for use in British coal mines.

Left: Working on the upper deck, as here on *U181*, was often fraught with considerable danger of being washed off and a good number of U-boat men lost their lives this way. Sometimes conditions were so rough that even the strong safety harnesses snapped. Non-essential work, such as reloading torpedoes from storage containers under the upper deck, was carried out when conditions allowed but repairs often took on a more urgent nature. One boat crossing the Atlantic found that its guns had been ripped off during a storm.

Below: U178 rolling through heavy seas, showing how difficult it was to gain access to the upper deck.

This page: U172, a Type IXC.

Right: Oberfunkmaat (Radio Petty Officer) Karl Günter, wearing wet weather gear while standing in for an ill colleague on *U67* in December 1941. The round device is the end of a speaking tube for giving directions to the helmsman down below in the central control room.

Above: Most pictures of U-boats were taken while close to port, when the crew could be allowed out on the upper deck, but this gives a somewhat false image of what conditions were like at sea.

Above: Although historians have projected a strong image of U-boats striking terror in the shipping lanes, the vast majority of them never came within shooting distance of the enemy. In fact, from a total of 1,171 U-boats, 674 never sunk anything throughout the entire war. Instead they became targets for the opposition, with many sinking during their first or second operational voyage. These depth charges dropped on *U848*, a Type IXD2 under Wilhelm Rollmann, fell wide of their mark and did nothing more than irritate and frighten the men inside.

Left: U534 on display in Birkenhead (England) showing the result of more accurate depth charge detonations. The sides have been so severely buckled that parts of the pressure hull have been ripped away from their supports, tearing a hole in the side and thus allowing seawater to pour in.

This page: These remarkable photographs were taken in the Mediterranean while the destroyers HMS *Hasty* and *Hotspur* were sinking *U79* on 23 December 1941. The Royal Navy also succeeded in rescuing every member of the crew, probably giving them the best Christmas present of their lives. *U79* was brought to the surface (below) but was still making headway while men were abandoning their stricken boat.

Above: The destroyers stood by, picking up men and wondering whether a small boat with boarding party might make it across to the wreck.

Above: Conditions were too rough for small boats and, in any case, it quickly became apparent that the U-boat was rapidly sinking. The Royal Navy watched men jump overboard until there was just one person left. Doggedly and faithful until the bitter end, one solitary man, Kptlt Wolfgang Kaufmann, remained on the top of the conning tower, gripping the rails and staring over to the nearby ship. It was not until water was washing around his feet that he jumped off, to swim over to the ship which had almost killed him.

Above: Kptlt Wolfgang Kaufmann, commander of *U79* and the last man to be rescued, grabbing a lifebelt thrown down to him.

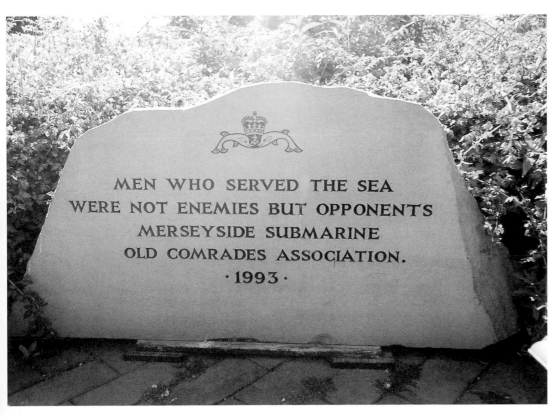

MEN WHO SERVED THE SEA
WERE NOT ENEMIES BUT OPPONENTS
MERSEYSIDE SUBMARINE
OLD COMRADES ASSOCIATION.
· 1993 ·

Left: It is surprising that U-boat men were rescued, despite the most appalling natural conditions. The reason why so many made the effort, and at times even risked their own lives to save the opposition, is perhaps best explained by this memorial outside the U-Boot-Archiv in Cuxhaven.

Chapter 6
The Secret Capture

U110 — The Victim

The commander of *U110*, Fritz-Julius Lemp, was born in Tsingtao (as it was then known, now usually Qingdao) on the shores of the Yellow Sea in northern China a year before World War 1. At first glance this may appear to be a long way from the naval ports in Germany, but psychologically it was a good deal closer than some of the land-locked towns of Bavaria, say. Tsingtao was Germany's equivalent of Britain's Hong Kong and had been 'leased' towards the end of the 19th century. In 1914 Tsingtao was a thriving sea port and the base for Germany's Far Eastern Cruiser Squadron under the com-

mand of Admiral Maximilian Reichsgraf von Spee. Spee and most of his ships would eventually be hunted down in the Battle of the Falkland Islands. Tsingtao was also the port from which the *Emden* sailed on her incredible raid on Allied merchant shipping in the Pacific and Indian Oceans.

From this background of eastern maritime romance, Lemp grew up in Germany and joined the still tiny Reichsmarine as an officer candidate at the age of 18 in 1931, two years before Hitler became Chancellor. He had hardly received his full commission when the opportunity presented itself to abandon a possible career in prestigious surface ships to become a member of Commodore Karl Dönitz's 'Freikorps', as the new U-boat flotilla had been nicknamed. Lemp first served as watch officer in the newly commissioned *U28* (Kptlt Wilhelm Ambrosius) but less than two years later he was given command of *U30*.

World War 2 was only a few hours old when *U30*, guided by Lemp's natural aggressiveness, achieved a notorious place in history by sinking the passenger ship *Athenia*. Not only did Lemp's uncontrolled enthusiasm get the better of him to act against orders, but he also dealt a severe blow against his own country by giving the British the excuse to engage in unrestricted sea warfare. But then, in many ways, the propaganda systems in Germany and Britain were more to blame than Lemp himself. He was responsible for the loss of a ship with over a hundred lives but it was in the political arena that both sides blew the incident out of all proportion. Incidentally, it is not true that Lemp sunk the first ship of the war. He was just the first U-boat commander to have done that. The Royal Navy had already upstaged him by sinking the German freighter *Olinda* off South America. She fell foul of the cruiser *Ajax* (Capt Charles Woodhouse), which later took part in the famous Battle of the River Plate against the pocket battleship *Admiral Graf Spee*.

On the way home from his first war cruise, Lemp initiated something which, unknowingly at the time, was going to change the way in which future generations recorded history. Peering first at a photo of his fox-terrier, Schnurzl, he looked up and called over to Georg Högel in the radio room to ask whether it was possible to paint a picture of the dog on the conning tower. Högel agreed to look for some paint for he, too, was missing the friendly little dog which had often accompanied them to sea. Somehow the presence of the animal added a calming atmosphere to the military sharpness of the submarine. Högel found some paint as well as a good supply of brushes and by the time *U30* moored in Wilhelmshaven

*Above: Fritz-Julius Lemp's first command (*U30*) was also a Type VIIA from Deschimag AG Weser in Bremen. The type can easily be identified in the photograph because it was the only one with an above-water torpedo tube at the rear. The number on the conning tower indicates that this photograph was taken before the beginning of hostilities and the red and white heads on the torpedoes confirm that the warheads are practice dummies without explosives.*

Above: U30 coming into Wilhelmshaven shortly after the beginning of the war. The heavy cruiser Admiral Hipper is in the background. Note that the number has been removed, but that the dog emblem has been painted on the side of the conning tower. This still has the old, straight prewar shape without the wave or spray deflector half-way up the tower.

there was a picture of the dog on both sides of the conning tower. Dönitz liked the touch, although he decreed that the emblem must be removed before the next operation, to prevent the opposition from identifying the boat at sea. Högel was an apt person to have been chosen to execute the painting. He had studied art in Munich but, like the Führer himself, he had found employment as an artist difficult and chose to overcome the problem by signing on in the navy. He never had any great liking for radios, but naval selection tests suggested that should be his calling.

That first professional painting of Schnurzl started a fad which was to snowball throughout the war. Dönitz's instructions to remove all forms of identification at sea were ignored and the emblems on conning towers have helped many historians by making it possible to identify otherwise virtually featureless grey hulks in old photographs. By the end of the war there must have been thousands of emblems which had been painted on conning towers, many of which have been recorded in Högel's own excellent book on the subject.

The sinking of the *Athenia* and the drawing on the conning tower were not the only 'firsts' in which *U30* played a part. She also later became the first U-boat to run into a French Atlantic port for refuelling. This happened on 7 July 1940 in Lorient. From there *U30* sailed southwards, to sink a tiny 726-ton freighter, the SS *Elleroy*. Despite this success, the operational days of *U30* were

numbered by this time. The machinery could no longer cope with the rigours of war and, like other Type VIIA boats, *U30* was nearing the end of its operational life. Consequently, Lemp refuelled once more in Lorient and then took a wide sweep through Britain's Western Approaches, past the North Channel, to lay his boat to rest in Wilhelmshaven. From there *U30* sailed to Kiel to be used for training in the Baltic.

Lemp succeeded in taking a few days' leave before making his way to Deschimag AG Weser in Bremen, to collect a brand-new and much larger boat. So far the war had made little impact on the town. Air raids had already started influencing life there, but in 1940 they were still infrequent and light enough to be irritating nuisances rather than deadly threats. Rather than breaking the civilian population, the raids had actually increased its resolve and Lemp was aware of a unified defiance which made the workers at the shipyard determined to get their boats quickly into the water.

With his Knight's Cross around his neck, Lemp stood out in the crowds to become the centre of attention wherever he went. This award was still a rarity during the autumn of 1940 and anyone wearing one received instant

VIP treatment. Lemp was only the eighth U-boat commander to have been awarded a Knight's Cross. He received his for persistent hard work when he reached the coveted 100,000 tons sunk just 10 days after Otto Kretschmer, the most successful commander of the war. The first Knight's Cross had gone to Günther Prien 10 months earlier for sinking the battleship *Royal Oak* in Scapa Flow. This indicates that the awards were not handed out like confetti, as has been claimed by some postwar authors, and it was indeed a great achievement to receive such a prestigious medal, making Lemp a member of a highly respected and tiny elite. Lemp was also one of the few commanders who had attacked and damaged an enemy battleship, HMS *Barham*, though its armour proved too strong for his torpedoes on that occasion. (*Barham*, however, was sunk by *U331* in the Mediterranean in November 1941.)

The major move, after commissioning *U110* in Bremen, was to take the boat into the Baltic for trials but *U110* did not remain there long. It was a bitterly cold February day in 1941 when the boat was made fast in Kiel for final fitting out and finishing off of a few minor repairs. The procedure ran like well-oiled clockwork because the 5th U-boat Flotilla had been especially created to take care of this, by providing everything new boats needed. Finally, on Sunday 9 March 1941, still an uncomfortably cold day but with spring in the air, *U110* cast off for her first

war voyage. The plans had been to sweep through Lemp's old hunting grounds of the Western Approaches and then make for Lorient in France, but initially it looked as if this might be frustrated. Two days earlier, Lemp had received instructions to make room for a passenger and such secret occurrences were often accompanied by odious orders to undertake something unpalatable. In the end it turned out not to have been terribly secret at all. *U110* was to take an enthusiastic construction worker to sea so that he could get the feel of what it was like to be in action.

Ulrich Kruse, an employee of the U-boat Acceptance Command, had made several applications to go to sea, but as an important worker in an essential position his efforts had always been frustrated because his bosses knew he could not easily be replaced. As a result, considerable string-pulling and undercover persuasion were necessary before he was given permission to accompany *U110* on her first war cruise. Yet, although he had succeeded in getting on board, Kruse remained well out of the way until the low German coastline and the prominent church towers of Cuxhaven were out of sight. He did not want to prompt anyone into getting the idea of

Below: U30 with a slightly modified conning tower. The wave or spray deflector has been added half-way up, but the later type of upper deflector has not yet been fitted. This photograph was taken in the massive sea locks at Wilhelmshaven.

Above: U30 returning to a hero's welcome in Wilhelmshaven. There were a number of different locks, dating back to various times in history. The last ones were built during the war when it was realised that the battleship *Tirpitz*, being built on the landward side of the locks, was about 10cm too wide to fit through them. This gave the navy the choice of either scrapping the battleship or building another set of slightly larger locks.

Left: Konteradmiral Karl Dönitz with Fritz-Julius Lemp not yet wearing his Knight's Cross. Therefore this photograph was taken before the end of August 1940, but after October 1939 when Dönitz was promoted. Since Lemp is wearing identical clothes to the ones in the next picture, it would suggest that this was taken shortly before he was awarded the Knight's Cross on 14 August 1940.

setting him ashore. His eagerness to learn everything about the machinery endeared him to the crew, who quickly gave him the honorary rank of Senior Staff Engineer. Edging out of the Elbe estuary was no easy matter and Kruse hardly appreciated the men's anxiety until the boat lurched sideways through the silvery moonlight to avoid the first mine. There were plenty more to follow.

Several uneventful days passed until silence was ordered while *U110* plunged down to a depth of 30 metres to hear what was going on. Conditions were good and ships could be heard over considerably longer distances than the lookouts could see them from the top of the conning tower. *U110* was in luck. Prominent propeller noises were heard before the first hour was up. Without hesitation Lemp surfaced, ordered the engines to high speed and shortly afterwards was rewarded with the sight of a convoy. Peering over the high conning tower wall, Kruse counted five columns, each about half a kilometre from the other. To his surprise neither Lemp nor the other officers were concentrating on this mass. Instead they were peering into the empty darkness. It was not until someone loaned him a pair of binoculars that he could see they were focusing on tiny, fast moving escorts — three of them.

Having assessed the situation, Lemp told his men that he was going in. The first torpedo was aimed at the leading ship on their side, a 5,000-tonner. Following this shot, the first watch officer, who aimed torpedoes during surface attacks, was ordered to turn his attention to a 10,000-ton tanker. Lemp did not seem to be doing anything. Standing there in grim silence, he merely watched what was going on. In fact he had no need to give any

orders; everybody knew what to do. However, things did not work out too well. Someone aboard the tanker must have spotted the U-boat. Suddenly it turned on to a ramming course, avoiding the torpedo and missing *U110* by only a hundred metres or so. Kruse, who felt the boat's rocking increase dramatically as it rolled over the tanker's wake, now realised why Lemp wore the Knight's Cross. With iron nerve, he merely ordered the first officer to shoot a torpedo from one of the rear tubes. The result was devastating. The tanker, with highly volatile petrol on board, seemed to vaporise as it flew into the air with an impressively brilliant ball of bright fire.

Star shells, for illuminating the black night, were not necessary and the escorts were not asleep either. *U110* crashed down, hoping to reach a safe depth before the first depth charges detonated. Nothing can be more terrifying than being at the receiving end of a depth charge attack, but Kruse came through his baptism of fire without injury, nor was there any damage to the boat. Luckily it was a short experience and about half an hour later Lemp was demonstrating how he had become one of Germany's top U-boat commanders. While returning to the surface, the silence above *U110* erupted once more into activity. Propeller noises became audible in the boat without need of the sensitive sound detection gear. Obviously the character upstairs was sitting there, listening and waiting for the U-boat to make its next move. Lemp was not deterred. With the motors running silently, he crept away for another half hour and then the cold dampness of the Atlantic was once more blown through the interior. Lemp was ready for his second attack.

He lined up a new target and two torpedoes vanished into the night but the tanker continued on its way undisturbed. The next two brought it to a standstill, but without the brilliant ball of fire seen earlier. Instead, the tanker just settled in the water, looking as if it was disappearing behind the horizon. It was not until it had gone down and the coming of daylight put an end to surface attacks that Lemp was told about the torpedoes' depth control mechanism having been filled with the wrong type of oil, which made them run slow and erratically. Other than curse, there was not much anyone could do about it, but the men were pleased enough with the bag for one night.

Kruse and the rest of Lemp's crew were lucky to have survived. *U99* (Kptlt Otto Kretschmer) and *U100* (Kptlt Joachim Schepke) had been sunk while *U110* was trimmed low in the water, examining wreckage floating on the restless Atlantic. Lemp knew that *U99* had been sunk because Kretschmer transmitted a distress call but there was nothing he could do. The lookouts aboard *U110* probably even watched the rescue attempt, but the best Lemp could manage was to retreat into the blackness of the vast Atlantic, hoping he would not become the escorts' third victim.

Later, Lemp turned his attention on a 5,000-tonner heading west, but despite all his experience and the torpedoes having been double-checked, they still failed to do their jobs. Coming after a long day's chase this failure was especially infuriating. Lemp had the necessary vocabulary to express his feelings and, at the same time as swearing, ordered the gun crews on deck. Both the 37mm quick-firing gun aft of the conning tower and the much larger 105mm forward were to bring the matter to a successful end. The smaller gun was the first to score a few hits, but these were so insignificant that there was no observable response. Then, when the larger ammunition

Above: This massive container port by the mouth of the River Weser had not yet been built when *U110* nosed down the river for the first time on her way to the training grounds in the Baltic, but the natural hazards in the river have hardly changed.

Above: The estuary of the River Elbe, looking from close to the U-Boot-Archiv in Cuxhaven-Altenbruch over to the entrance of the Kiel Canal at Brunsbüttel. The river looks exceptionally wide at this point, but the deep water channel is narrow and most of this water is not deep enough to float even a submarine at most tidal states.

was brought up, everybody was surprised by a louder than normal bang. Peering over the conning tower wall, after their ears had cleared, it became obvious that the 105mm had been fired without first removing the watertight tampion at the end. Even the men inside the boat knew something untoward had happened. Several fuses on the ceiling of the radio room, immediately below the gun, dropped out of their fittings and light bulbs were smashed. Radio operator Georg Högel was not a happy man with reverberations ringing in his ears for some time, making it difficult to hear what was going on in the airwaves.

Above: Despite the natural hazards, the Rivers Elbe, Weser and many other harbour approaches were protected by massive anti-submarine nets. This tiny relic is now on display in the U-Boot-Archiv.

Above: Part of the anti-submarine net which used to protect the River Elbe, now on display at the Wreck Museum in Cuxhaven.

Despite all this chaos around him, Lemp barked down the voice pipes for more speed. There were still torpedoes in the tubes and he was going to have another go at the target. Inside the boat, men felt the increased vibration from the diesels thumping away. Suddenly, and most unexpectedly, the engines stopped. Everything went quiet while the boat settled into a smoother rolling on the restless waves. No one inside knew that the men on the conning tower stood horrified, staring at the foredeck. Instead of lifting up above the waves, one side had dropped down to such a precarious angle that it was threatening to wash the lookouts off the conning tower. Thinking that someone had accidentally opened the forward diving tanks, Lemp ordered them to be blown. A mass of bubbling foam emerging from under the deck made it obvious that something untoward had happened. At last Kruse was able to repay the men of *U110* for their warm hospitality. Having worked with the Submarine Acceptance Command for three years he was well acquainted with the intricacies of piping running through diving tanks and could help in repairing the damage. This did not look good enough for another hunt nor for diving, but it did keep the boat afloat

and saved the men from going for an early enforced swim. Crawling back at a painfully slow speed, *U110* eventually reached Lorient where there were excellent repair facilities.

Kruse had to make his own way back to Germany, but the experience had been more than worth it. He brought back numerous small ideas for making the boats more efficient. He had been to war, survived a depth charge attack, was not hurt when the gun exploded and then, ironically when he was just a few kilometres from his destination in Kiel, he almost lost his life during an air attack on his train. The voyage with *U110* had been an unforgettable experience. Yet, despite the hardships, Kruse wished he could have participated in one more trip, to become eligible for the highly prestigious U-boat badge. I am grateful to him for having left a report of his experiences in the U-boat Archive.

Lemp's State of Mind

In order to understand why *U110* would shortly be abandoned in such a hurry by one of the most experienced and combative commanders, it is necessary to look back at what was going through his mind at the time. As well as his own troubles with torpedoes, Lemp would have known that other U-boats had had similar difficulties. Some boats had even been lost because of this and the vital information had been sent back to Germany by survivors from prisoner of war camps through a secret letter code. The next of kin of some key officers had been informed to forward mail from prisoners to the Naval High Command, where the hidden messages were extracted from apparently innocuous personal notes. This is explained in Appendix V.

Throughout the autumn of 1940, U-boat successes had been incredibly frequent while only one or two boats were lost each month. What is more, no boats at all had been lost during January and February 1941. These odds encouraged commanders like Lemp to steer closer to the wind and perhaps take risks which they would have avoided earlier. Lemp knew that his boat could go faster on the surface than the majority of escorts, that it was difficult for the British to spot a surfaced U-boat on a dark night and, even when submerged, he was likely to be faced with a few half-hearted depth charge attacks and then would be left alone. In fact, frequently the frightful pinging of the Asdic was worse than the far-off detonations. The reason for this was that the small number of escorts were required around the convoys and could not be spared to kill U-boats. Their orders were to compel the U-boats to submerge and then return as quickly as possible to the merchant ships, hoping that the Germans would lose contact while they were below the surface. The terrific confidence which all this instilled in U-boat crews received its first knock during those first two months of 1941, when successes dropped off quite remarkably. Yet, this was not due to attacks being fouled up; it was caused by U-boats being unable to find convoys. The idea of spies contributing to this state of affairs crossed the minds of many and consequently several procedures were reviewed to eradicate any possible leaks. It very much looked like a temporary setback.

Then suddenly there was a spate of casualties. Schepke's *U100* and Kretschmer's *U99* were both lost, as we have seen, in attacking convoy HX112 and Lemp himself was ultimately driven away by the escorts. The incidents of that fateful night left many in *U110* with plenty of food for thought. During those emotional minutes, just before dropping off to sleep, many realised that they were living on borrowed time. Lemp and his men would also have heard about the serious damage incurred by *U37* (Kptlt Nico Clausen) when it was rammed while attacking convoy HX112 just one day before Kretschmer and Schepke were sunk. And this was not the end of the story. Several other similar tales of destroyers bearing down on U-boats at great speed were circulating, indicating that being rammed was indeed becoming a serious possibility. Lemp had hardly reached Lorient with his damaged boat when it became apparent that the heroes of Scapa Flow in *U47* under Kptlt Günther Prien were not going to make it home either. This was not all; *U70* (Kptlt Joachim Matz) had also gone down at the beginning of the month and *U551* (Kptlt Karl Schrott) followed on 23 March, less than a week before *U110* crawled back into Lorient. *U76* (Oberleutnant-zur-See [ObltzS] Friedrich von Hippel) followed shortly after.

U-boat commanders knew that it was becoming increasingly difficult to locate targets and could sense that the escorts were becoming more persistent in driving home their attacks. So far, as we have noted, the escorts' main brief had been to put U-boats down and then return as quickly as possible to the protective screen around the convoy. Early in 1941, this tactic began to be changed. Escort commanders were encouraged to engage in longer hunts and it was even suggested that they might also consider capturing a U-boat. But it was strongly emphasised that such action should only be contemplated if the conditions were right. Getting back into position around the merchant ships was still a high priority.

In April *U110* left for her second war voyage, knowing that life in the Atlantic had suddenly become highly precarious. Lemp had come within a whisker of also having gone down, but somehow this thought was pushed to the back of his mind until a few days later when he saw the grey bows of an enemy escort bearing down. On that fateful day when Lemp was faced with white foam shearing away from the destroyer's bows as it aimed itself at *U110*, he knew that there was no escape and his only course of action was to save his men.

Minutes earlier, *U110* had been in tiptop condition, with batteries and compressed air bottles filled to maximum for a submerged attack. Everything was calm. Three torpedoes shot out of the bow tubes, the compensating tanks were flooding efficiently, keeping the boat below the surface, when Lemp suddenly ordered 'go deep as quickly as possible' in his usual quiet and calm voice. He was sitting on his saddle inside the conning tower control room and the engineering officer, ObltzS (Ing) Hans-Joachim Eichelborn, down below by the hydroplane operators, had no idea what was going on outside. The bows of the boat had just started tipping down and men were still rushing forwards, to make the bows heavier, when the first set of depth charges struck. The force of the detonations smashed the main control panel for the electric motors, which refused to work even after the switches had been put back to their correct positions. All depth gauges in the central control room and in the bow torpedo room smashed, chlorine gas filled the boat so that the men had to don their breathing apparatus, fuel cell number 4 was torn open on the inside and several valves failed. The situation looked grim, but Eichelborn was no beginner. He ordered pressure gauges to be fitted on the main cooling water inlets for the diesel engines and therefore ascertained that the boat was not dropping down into dangerous depths. The trim was excellent, which was just as well because hydroplane controls as well as the electric rudder failed. The boat was certainly not going to evade another depth charge attack. As damage reports flooded in, it became clear that at least one of the propeller shafts had been bent, but no one could examine that area because it was filling rapidly with water. The situation was grim. *U110* had come to the end. This time there was no escape. Lemp ordered the boat to surface. Jumping up on the bridge, he ordered the men out.

The Convoy System in Early 1941

The general principle at this stage of the war was for westbound convoys, like OB318, to sail with escorts from Britain until they were south of Iceland, at which point the escorts would have to refuel. There they would be relieved by another escort group based in Iceland until the merchant ships were clear of U-boat infested waters. At that point, in the far western reaches of the Atlantic, the merchant ships would disperse and continue on alone. (Later in 1941 convoys would be escorted throughout their routes.) Going in the other direction, the convoy would assemble at some far distant anchorage, such as Halifax in Canada, and sail unprotected until it was met at the Western Ocean Meeting Point by an escort group from Iceland which would usually have just left a group of merchant ships going in the opposite direction. These warships would then accompany the convoy to the Eastern Ocean Meeting Point, where they would meet another group which had come from Britain with an outward-bound convoy. This whole process was later made more effective by refuelling escorts from a tanker in the convoy.

Convoy OB318

Convoy OB318 sailed northwards from Liverpool in the early afternoon of 2 May 1941, but remained in the Minches off northern Scotland for the next three days until all the merchant ships were assembled. At first the convoy was accompanied by the 7th Escort Group under the command of Cdr I. H. Bockett-Pugh together with part of the 3rd Escort Group. The plan, in line with the system outlined above, was for the remainder of the 3rd, under Capt Joe Baker-Cresswell, to sail from Iceland and take over the mid-ocean part of the route. The 7th Escort Group would turn back at that point. In the end this meeting produced a mixture of feelings among the cumbersome merchant ships because Baker-Cresswell brought along a surprise in the form of a large passenger ship converted into an armed merchant cruiser. Some thought its huge size would attract U-boats and thereby endanger the smaller ships, while others were of the opinion that the enemy would be more likely to concentrate on the giant rather than attempt tackling the smaller ships.

7th Escort Group (Cdr Bockett-Pugh)

Destroyers:	*Westcott*
	Campbelltown
	Newmarket
Sloop:	*Rochester*
Corvettes:	*Auricula*
	Dianthus
	Marigold
	Nasturtium
	Primrose

3rd Escort Group (Cdr Baker-Cresswell)

Destroyers:	*Bulldog*
	Amazon
	Broadway
Corvettes:	*Aubrietia*
	Hollyhock
	Nigella
Armed trawlers:	*Angle*
	Daneman
	St Apollo
Armed merchant cruiser:	*Ranpura*

OB318's initial progress was uneventful and it passed the first stage without serious incident. Half a year earlier these waters immediately to the west of Scotland had been the U-boats' main hunting grounds, but now it was noticeable that the Germans had been driven further west. The only real excitement came a day out from the Minches, when lookouts in the sloop *Rochester* sighted something grey floating just below the surface of the water. Upon closer examination it was found to be a stationary torpedo. Excitement grew when it was realised that it was German and would make an ideal present for the technical boys back home. Consequently HMS *Westcott* stopped to pick it up.

OB318 was marked on the German command map as *U110's* convoy two hours before midnight of 8/9 May 1941. *U94* (Kptlt Herbert Kuppisch) had also sighted the same convoy, but initial confusion made the staff officers in the U-boat Command at Kernevel, near Lorient in western France, think that two groups of merchant ships instead of one had been found. The radio room in Lorient was not the only recipient of the news. *U201* (Kptlt Adalbert Schnee) and *U556* (Kptlt Herbert Wohlfarth) ordered their engines on to fast cruising speed with the hope of getting in on the action.

From this point in the proceedings it is a little difficult to determine exactly what happened. Every report is slightly different and the problem is compounded by the earlier German misconception that they were chasing two convoys rather than one. However, an exact reconstruction of the sequence of events is hardly necessary to appreciate the U-boat commanders' concerns. On the one hand they were hoping that the escorts would run short of fuel and leave; on the other they had to consider their own oil consumption and therefore did not wish to be drawn too far west. Fear of losing the merchant ships, together with the U-boat Command's earlier order to attack at once, drove them into immediate action.

Below:
The Liverpool skyline seen from Birkenhead just six months before the end of the 20th century. Although there are a good number of new buildings, men who left with Convoy OB318 in May 1941 would still recognise the prominent landmarks. Liverpool had the biggest docks on the English west coast and also housed the command centre for the Western Approaches and the Atlantic. Accommodated inside a well-protected bunker within the cellar of Derby House, it is now open as a museum.

Above: A convoy seen from the air. Tell-tale wakes indicate that columns of sluggish merchant ships are slowly moving from right to left.

Below: HMS *Broadway* assisted in the capture of *U110*. Imperial War Museum

The Day of the Capture

It was about 0830 hours on 9 May when Baker-Cresswell appeared on *Bulldog's* bridge with a view to settling into the day routine for the last hours with the convoy. The 3rd Escort Group under his command was almost within sight of Greenland, in an area so far not frequented by U-boats, but there was enough fuel for another 10 hours or so plus a generous safety reserve for the escorts to reach Iceland for refuelling. Baker-Cresswell decided to remain with the merchant ships until mid-afternoon of that day. The convoy had only a short while earlier passed beyond the maximum range of Icelandic air cover, but had there been an aircraft in the sky, it would have spotted two U-boats closing in on each other for a discussion through loudhailers. Lying just over the convoy's northerly horizon meant they could not be seen by any of the merchant ships. One of these submarines was Lemp's *U110* and the other Schnee's *U201*. Lemp's officers were of the opinion that they should continue shadowing until the escorts left. Perhaps a good suggestion, but not one which appealed to Lemp nor Schnee. Lemp had not gained his Knight's Cross by hanging around and Schnee

was awarded the same prestigious award three months after this meeting, suggesting that he was not a cautious type either. It was decided that Lemp should go in first for a submerged attack in daylight and *U201* would follow a short while later.

U110's torpedoes were shot two minutes before midday, when Baker-Cresswell was standing on his bridge, shooting the sun for an accurate noon fix of his position. The first indication of something untoward happening was the sight of a column of water rising up to spray over the *Esmond*, the lead ship of the right-hand column. This caused her deck cargo of vehicles to be spilled into the sea as if some giant was throwing toys around. The dull thud of the detonation had hardly reached *Bulldog's* bridge when another column of water shot high into the air. This time *Bengore Head*, further towards the middle of the convoy, was hit. The men of the convoy stared in disbelief, initially not grasping that they had come under attack. U-boats had never reached this far west and somehow everything seemed unreal, almost as if it were a dream. Yet, the escorts reacted exceptionally quickly. Despite *Esmond* going down exceedingly fast, her crew launched lifeboats and everybody got off, virtually without getting wet. Long before the men were pulling on their oars to get away from the wreck, the escorts had already started taking retaliatory action.

HMS *Aubrietia* (Lt-Cdr V. F. Smith) was guarding the flank from which Lemp attacked. The high-pitched screams of the torpedo engines were heard before the impressive sight of the detonations openly announced the presence of a submerged submarine. As a result, depth charges were already erupting by the time the torpedoes

Above: Jimmy White of SS *York City*, a few years before the beginning of the war. A good number of ships were still coal fired, meaning that they had teams of burly boilermen constantly shovelling fuel into hungry furnaces. Work aboard such ships was arduous and dirty.

Above: Coaling was always an essential part of the time spent in ports and most breaks in voyages were dictated by the need to take on fuel. Usually it was shovelled into the bunkers by gangs of colliers who did not go to sea with the ship. This gave the crew some respite, but it still left the boat covered with a good layer of fine black dust which found its way into all crooks and crannies.

found their mark. Most men aboard *Aubrietia* did not think these could have had much effect, but that did not prevent them throwing a second pattern a few minutes later. The virtually instant response must have had a shattering effect upon Lemp and his crew. He almost certainly had not counted on being at the receiving end of a depth charge attack before his torpedoes had even struck. Despite suffering a breakdown of her Asdic gear, *Aubrietia* severely crippled the U-boat. Lights went out, gauges burst, water squirted in and there was pandemonium in the confined darkness.

Aubrietia's breakdown hardly mattered, for both *Bulldog* and *Broadway* had gained Asdic contact and were racing towards the suspected spot when their lookouts saw an eerie eruption ahead, almost as if some monster were stirring the water from below the surface. A short while later, *U110* surfaced. *Bulldog* immediately went on to a ramming course, but this order had hardly been executed when Baker-Cresswell realised a capture might come off. Ordering the engines in reverse, he brought his ship to a standstill some hundred metres from the stricken enemy. Seeing *Broadway* still charging ahead he instructed the signal 'Keep Clear' to be flashed while he even shouted through the megaphone, although he must have known that no one on *Broadway* could have heard him.

It transpired later that *Broadway* was intending to drop another set of depth charges to prevent the boat from diving, but this misfired. Depth charges did erupt, but the ship did not come to a halt. Instead it struck a glancing blow against the submarine. This might not have been too serious had the submarine's hydroplanes not stuck out sideways below the surface. Hitting these caused a wide gash to be torn in the forward fuel bunkers, covering the whole area in foul-smelling oil. So, although *Broadway* may have messed up her part in the action, she

Below: The lads aboard SS *Bradburn* in June 1934, a British merchant ship being loaded with fuel in Cardiff for another long voyage.

probably contributed to the men in *U110* abandoning their boat rather quickly. The U-boat crew began emerging into the open, ready, as we now know, to abandon ship, though the British were not yet fully aware of this. All this happened exceedingly fast and an impressive display of gunfire further encouraged the men to abandon *U110* rather than stand about on deck.

While *Broadway* was nursing her wounds and trying to recover some pride, *Aubrietia* was busy picking up the men from torpedoed freighter *Esmond*. Having done this, she manoeuvred into this cauldron of activity to rescue the Germans, who were taken below so quickly that they could not watch what was going on. None of them saw the whaler from *Bulldog* carrying an armed boarding party to the U-boat.

As so often happened, various misunderstandings led to unfortunate incidents. Two Germans, for example, staggered out of the conning tower and on to the forward deck, where they grabbed hold of the gun for support only to find themselves being mown down because the British thought they were going to shoot back. Another man, collapsing into the arms of a rescuer aboard *Aubrietia*, threw up a mouthful of seawater only to find himself being hurled back into the sea. Apparently the seaman helping him thought he was being spat at.

One aspect of what happened has been wrapped in considerable confusion. It has been suggested that this was due to a British attempt to conceal a cold-blooded murder. Reliable sources in Germany who have interviewed some of the men from the boarding party and located a confidential report have suggested that Lemp was shot while trying to reboard his stricken boat. Yet, it is exceedingly difficult to fit this possible scenario into the order of events and even the German evidence fails to support such a shooting.

Above: The officer of the watch peering over a calm, serene sea shortly before the outbreak of the war.

Above: SS *Bradburn* of 4,736 tons in September 1932, a year before Hitler came to power, showing the type of ships which made up the convoys of World War 2.

A few minutes before, Lemp had apparently vacated his seat by the periscope inside the conning tower shortly after having given the order to dive deep. He closed the pressure resistant hatch in the roof of the control room, jumped down and was standing by the depth controls when the first depth charges threw him off his feet. Men observed traces of blood on his forehead, but he seemed fit enough to take charge. He had probably received quite a battering, however, so he was not in the best of condition when the time came to abandon ship, and swimming in the cold water would have sapped even more energy from him. His mind was obviously still functioning because later he told a number of men, including the first watch officer, ObltzS Dietrich Loewe, to swim back to the boat to reboard and scuttle it, but the wind was blowing *U110* away from them. Loewe later told Dönitz that this attempt to reboard did not bring them any nearer to the boat, though some have suggested that Lemp was shot in the attempt. Whatever did happen, it is highly unlikely that those critical last minutes of Lemp's life will ever be clarified for certain.

The boarding party, under the command of Sub-Lieutenant David Balme, was made up of Able Seaman (AB) Cyril Dolley, AB Sydney Pearce, AB Richard Roe, AB Claude Wileman, Ordinary Seaman (OD) Arnold Hargreaves, OD John Trotter, Stoker Cyril Lee and Telegraphist Allen Long. They pulled straight over to the windward side of the U-boat because it was the nearest. With Baker-Cresswell's words ringing in his ears that it did not matter if he lost the whaler, Balme did not want to risk any delay while he took the time to move through the heavy swell to the calmer side. Boarding was made considerably easier than was first imagined because a wave washed the whaler on to *U110*'s deck, giving the men a scare and wedging it tight enough not to be moved without further assistance.

Climbing up to the top of the conning tower, Balme found the main hatch shut. He twisted the locking

Above: SS *Dallas City* slogging through a turbulent sea just six months before the beginning of the war.

Above: SS *Bradburn* chugging through 'green water' as the heavy waves were called.

Above: SS *Bradburn* at sea, rolling in turbulent waters.

Below: Although merchant ships were considerably bigger and sat higher in the water than tiny submarines, waves and spray still washed over them. This helped to remove the last traces of coal dust from the superstructure, but also made working on deck exceedingly unpleasant and rusted the ironwork.

Above: SS *Bradburn* being battered by a storm.

Above: It is highly likely that this is the 8,715-ton steamer *Natia* being sunk with a torpedo from the auxiliary cruiser *Thor* after the crew had been taken off on 8 October 1940.

mechanism, and had to jump back because the heavy springs automatically lifted the lid once the grip was released. Looking into the dim interior, he saw another similar closed hatch at the bottom. Climbing down with gas mask and large naval revolver was virtually impossible for anyone not accustomed to performing the act single-handed. So, hoping there was no one left on board, he holstered his gun and cautiously opened the hatch to the control room. The place seemed eerie and deserted, but there was no smell of gas so Balme discarded both weapon and gas mask and ordered that everything at hand should be passed up the ladder. Since no one could read German, the men only discarded what were obviously reading books for the crew's entertainment. Everything else, including a mass of useless material, was passed up. While this was going on, the radioman wrote down the frequency settings of the transmitters and receivers in the radio room.

Realising that the U-boat was not likely to sink in the next few minutes, Balme and his men instigated a more thorough search and made some attempt to stabilise the precarious angle at which *U110* was floating. None of them were submariners and therefore did not fancy pulling on any levers or turning the wheels. There was a good chance that the situation could be made worse. Since one of the engines was still running, it was decided to set its controls to the same position as the stationary one, but this had no effect. Possibly the stationary engine had been damaged because even with the controls set identically, the propellers on the other side continued churning very slowly.

While this was going on inside, another group on the outside had found the retractable bollards, raised them and then searched for a towing wire. This was stored in a locker which filled with water every time the boat dived and therefore the wire inside it was rather rusty. It looked too precarious to use as a tow attachment and in the end *Bulldog* came alongside to drop a hawser. This towing attempt went reasonably well until the wire caught on the U-boat's sharp casing and Balme decided to cast it off rather than risk damage. At that moment, just as things were looking good, came a spine-chilling cry of 'periscope in sight'. It was *U201*, making its attempt to get at the convoy, but luckily for the Royal Navy the boat was too far away to notice the commotion with the escorts. In any case, Schnee was not very interested in small warships as long as they did not prevent him from attacking. However, captured U-boat or not, *Bulldog* moved off to challenge the intruder and the men inside *U110* were treated to the horrific sound of depth charges detonating, a frightening noise even at such considerable distance.

In the meantime, Balme had plenty of opportunity to look around and his men started searching through other parts of the boat. They were surprised by the good quality clothing provided for their opposition and by the availability of attractive food. Later, Balme wrote in his report that there was nothing 'Ersatz' (wartime emergency) about any of the gear. The boat was clean, attractive,

with good fittings and the Germans had been well provided for. The searchers also found numbered keys for every locked cupboard, except one. Deciding that this must contain something important, it was gently broken open. Imagine the men's reaction when they discovered that they had just burst into the first aid box. Another group decided it would be worth removing some of the radio and sound detection gear, and carefully unscrewed the boxes from their positions. Carrying them into the central control room was not easy, nor was the attachment of a rope to pull them up the conning tower. But then, having put in all that effort, the men realised that they did not fit through the hatches.

Balme and his men had been aboard *U110* for well over five hours by the time *Bulldog* returned from her hunt. In that time they made a thorough search of the interior, taking not only essential items but also a few souvenirs. The tow was later reconnected and *Bulldog* made the effort to pull *U110* to Iceland. This went reasonably well until the following day. At 0400 hours the wind was still blowing from the southwest at force 4. Three hours later it had backed to come further from the south and the intensity had increased to force 6, meaning that both *Bulldog* and *U110* were rocking over considerable waves. The U-boat had been empty for some time, with hatches and pressure resistant doors tightly shut, and Baker-Cresswell even changed direction to run with the wind rather than being lashed sideways on, but all to no avail. Without much warning, at 1100 hours, *U110* started going down stern first. At one stage the bows stuck almost vertically out of the water, indicating that there was nothing which could be done other than cut the towing hawser. Losing the boat was a bitter blow.

On his return home a few days later, Baker-Cresswell received his reward when a man from Bletchley Park turned up with a briefcase to carry back the captured items. Realising that something more than a bag was needed, he assured Baker-Cresswell that this had been one of the most valuable actions of the whole war. Although the capture of an Enigma machine has often been cited as the most important part of this capture, this was not true because Britain already had several such machines and knew the wiring of the naval wheels necessary to operate it. Copies of several code books were the decisive part of this operation and made it possible for Bletchley Park to gain a massive insight into Kriegsmarine operations.

It had been a truly secret affair. Even the merchant ships in the convoy had not witnessed the capture, and now the chance of breaking into Enigma closed the shutters even more tightly. In fact, all information about the capture was duly removed from the usual records and placed under tight security. After the war, when Captain Roskill wrote his official history of the war at sea, he scarcely mentioned the sinking of *U110*. It was not until Baker-Cresswell told him about the capture that the whole matter came to light. Consequently, Roskill wrote the magnificent book, The Secret Capture, which was the only source of information for a long time, though when it was first published it did not explain any details about Enigma or codebreaking generally. Some authors have not only copied Roskill's information but also used exactly the same words without acknowledging the original source.

Above and below: Fires were quite a nuisance for submarines because smoke drifting up high into the sky often attracted unwelcome attention from aircraft or warships.

U110's first watch officer, ObltzS Dietrich Loewe, had a faint inkling that something out of the ordinary had happened. Everybody had raced out quickly when Lemp gave the order to abandon ship and no one had any recollections of scuttling charges being set. Georg Högel, the radio operator, said that one does not hang about when the order to abandon ship is given. Apparently Lemp was even questioned about the destruction of secret materials, but told his men to leave things where they were and get out fast.

Loewe ended up in the same Canadian prisoner of war camp as Otto Kretschmer where he quickly found enough experts to discuss the last moments of *U110*. First the letter code was used to report a possible capture and later Loewe feigned illness in order to get himself exchanged as a prisoner of war to bring this matter to the attention of the U-boat Command. However, by the time he reached Germany, he had changed his mind once more. Following more discussion, the consensus of opinion was that *U110* had indeed been sunk. There had been no news of a capture and even if the Enigma machine had been captured, the settings extracted from *U110* would soon have become outdated and of little use to the British.

Left: This poignant photograph drives home the bitterness of the war at sea and shows what a graveyard the restless Atlantic had become.

Below: The sinking of a freighter, showing what should have happened if German torpedoes had functioned properly. Magnetic pistols should have made them detonate under the merchant ship, thereby breaking it in half, but these frequently did not work and contact pistols had to be used instead. These detonated the torpedo by the side of the ship, creating the type of spray seen in the photograph on page 77. This would have torn a hole in the side, but not necessarily have sunk the ship.

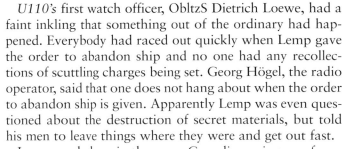

Chapter 7
The Surrender of *U570*

It was around noon on a bright but blustery August day in 1941 when a submarine surfaced among bubbling foam below Hudson 'S', being flown on anti-submarine reconnaissance south of Iceland by Squadron Leader J. H. Thompson. The bomber immediately dropped into a steep curving attack dive, straddling the target with four depth charges. While the bomber was regaining height, the crew were surprised to see a white flag fluttering on the conning tower. Meeting a stationary U-boat on the surface seemed unbelievable. Seeing a white flag of surrender was even more implausible. Yet, it was plain enough. The U-boat was surrendering, but there was nothing anyone could do to claim the prize. Even if the Hudson had been equipped with floats, the waves were too rough for landing. All Hudson 'S' could do was to ask for help, while it circled out of effective range of the puny anti-aircraft armament on the rear of the tower. This was a time when Type VIIC boats were still equipped with a single 20mm gun on the *Wintergarten*, aft of the conning tower; the single 88mm on the foredeck was too clumsy for use against aircraft. Some time before a shortage of fuel forced Hudson 'S' back to base in Iceland, another aircraft, this time a Catalina, took over the guard duty until ships from the Royal Navy arrived to tow the prize to Iceland. Eventually the boat, *U570*, was brought back to Britain to be commissioned into the Royal Navy as HMS *Graph*.

In the meantime, the German officers had arrived at a prisoner of war camp where their peers arranged a secret court martial for surrendering the boat. Both the commander, Kptlt Hans Rahmlow, and the first officer, LtsZ Bernhard Berns, were found guilty of cowardice in the face of the enemy, ostracised and told they would have to face a proper court martial once they returned to Germany. Wishing to redeem himself, the first officer volunteered to escape with a view to making for Barrow-in-Furness where *U570* was known to be lying. There he would try to get into the boat and scuttle her. However, he was captured by the Home Guard and shot.

This story in a nutshell has obviously been exploited to the fullest by every propaganda merchant in the business and the surrender, with a white flag fluttering from a U-boat, has continued to fascinate historians for years

Below: Hans-Joachim Rahmlow sitting behind the three beer bottles with the piston rings of a Kapitänleutnant, commander of *U570* when it was captured.

Above: Kptlt Rahmlow who surrendered *U570* to an aircraft in mid-Atlantic.

after the war. Consequently such vast number of variations, describing slightly different sequences of events, have appeared as to make it extremely difficult to separate fact from fiction. So, rather than contribute another possibly dubious version of the story, it might be better to look at the drama separately from Kptlt Rahmlow's and then the Royal Navy's point of view. This is possible because in bringing the matter to light during the mid-1950s, the German magazine *Kristall* generated such an immense postbag that several of the crew, who all wished to remain anonymous, wrote their version of what happened and this prompted Rahmlow to record how he had seen the surrender unfold. His account was published by *Kristall* verbatim as the last article of a fascinating series.

Hans-Joachim Rahmlow was indeed a remarkable character. He joined the Reichsmarine at the age of 19 in 1928, five years before Hitler came to power, at a time when it was exceedingly difficult to get into the army, even more arduous to become a naval officer and the Luftwaffe had not even been established. At the beginning of the war he commanded a land-based naval artillery unit and remained with heavy guns until early 1940. Although he was wearing a naval uniform, Rahmlow was very much a land sailor employed in locations where his men could theoretically shoot at ships.

From April 1940, Rahmlow went through submarine training for a period of five months before being apprenticed to Heinrich Bleichrodt in *U48*. Bleichrodt later commanded *U109*, the boat on which Wolfgang Hirschfeld was radio operator and which was used for the first radio-telephone conversation experiments, mentioned in the first chapter. *U48* was the most successful boat of

World War 2, so Rahmlow was in good hands, surrounded by the cream of the navy. The first watch officer, Reinhard Suhren, later became a successful commander of *U564* and then Flag Officer for U-boats — Norway as well as FdU, Nordmeer (Polar Seas). The second watch officer, Otto Ites, was also a well-known character and became commander of *U94*, the first boat to have a go at the convoy which was responsible for the capture of *U110*. There were two Iteses in the German submarine service. Otto had an identical twin brother Rudolf, who commanded *U709*. The LI (Engineering Officer), Erich Zürn, also became one of the most respected Knights of the Iron Cross and later served as engineering officer for 29th and then the 5th U-boat Flotilla.

Following one operational voyage with *U48*, Rahmlow was given command of *U58*, a small coastal boat of Type IIC. However, he did not go to war with this small dugout. She had already been retired from active service and was being used as a school boat in the Baltic. So, for four months, Rahmlow could sharpen his skills in the safety of the forgiving Baltic, where he was well out of reach of the opposition. His only enemies there were the boat itself, taskmasters from the navy and the natural elements. In April 1941, he appeared at Deutsche Werke in Kiel to learn about his new command and to weld his crew into shape. *U570* was commissioned on 15 May 1941 and, almost exactly three months later, she left the Baltic for Norway, called in on Trondheim and then sailed from there for her first operational cruise on 23 August 1941. In this short time there was no way *U570* could have been made truly ready for war. Anyone still searching for someone to blame for the wild surrender should look at the system which sent so many inexperienced men to face tasks and conditions they could hardly have imagined beforehand.

However inexperienced Rahmlow and his men may have been, he had sampled much of what the Atlantic, the Royal Navy and the RAF could throw at him. His voyage with *U48* was no pleasure cruise and he even experienced a full rehearsal of the events which later led to the capture of his own boat. This happened in October 1940, when *U48* was chasing a convoy through atrocious conditions. Bleichrodt's attention was concentrated on a destroyer, which had earlier forced him into the cellar when suddenly, without warning, a Sunderland dropped from the low clouds. The scream 'Alarm' bellowed down the tower at the same time as lookouts dropped on to the control room floor. The flying giant was less than two kilometres away when it was first spotted, meaning that it dropped its depth charges before *U48* could reach a safe depth. Two enormous detonations caused a violent shudder.

The usual commotion of bruised bodies collecting themselves from the bottom of the ladder had hardly subsided when another two violent detonations wreaked havoc in the dim interior. Whoever was up

Above and right: Before joining the U-boat arm, Rahmlow worked with a naval artillery unit, like this one near Le Havre in France. Although these huge guns could be aimed at ships, the conditions for working them were considerably different from the hazards faced by a rocking U-boat in the Atlantic.

there was not content with tickling the U-boat, and another two depth charges detonated fairly close by before the lookouts could reach their diving stations. It appeared as if the aircraft had called in reinforcements because then a salvo of five explosions followed. After that came another six and a short while later another six. Yet Bleichrodt did not allow himself to be ruffled, Suhren complained about noisy neighbours and Zürn continued issuing orders with the same calm he used when asking for another cup coffee or for someone to pass the salt at meal times.

Less than six hours later came a repeat performance. This time *U48* experienced seven separate attacks, during which a total of 26 depth charges were dropped. The damage to the interior was minimal and the men dealt with breakages as they occurred. Rahmlow therefore certainly knew what it felt like to be on the receiving end of a violent depth charge attack and, had he been paying attention, he would have seen that the blowing of tanks was not a good option. Instead Zürn lightened the load by using the massive, high pressure ballast pump to expel water which had penetrated the interior.

On that fateful August day when Rahmlow surfaced below Hudson 'S', it would seem that he failed to have a good look round first by periscope, though even then he might very well not have noticed the aircraft if it were immediately above him. Commander and some lookouts were already on the bridge by the time they spotted the danger. Being virtually stationary on the surface, *U570* took the best part of a minute to get under again and was straddled with depth charges before it reached a safe depth. This blast caused the glass in instruments to shatter and depth gauges to smash. Jets of water squirted into the interior until the taps in connecting pipes were turned off. At the same time batteries were damaged and water penetrated the bow compartment. The damage to the depth gauges was the most serious because there was no way of telling the depth as *U570* plummeted down, meaning there was a good chance of dropping below the deepest safety depth. Without consulting his engineering officer, Rahmlow ordered the diving tanks to be blown with compressed air. This halted the downward movement, but also resulted in an uncontrollable upward acceleration, with the boat increasing speed as the water pressure on the outside became less. Rahmlow was now under the impression that his boat was unfit for diving and that the interior was filling with poisonous gases. In fact his account states that even a day later the Royal Navy could only get inside by wearing breathing apparatus.

In his account Rahmlow also emphasised that there were only two experienced men aboard and the ignorance of the rest resulted in some unfortunate actions being taken without his instructions. The first happened when a lookout pulled out a towel he was using as a scarf to wave it at the aircraft in the hope of preventing a second attack. Rahmlow immediately told the man to stop because it could be mistaken for a white flag of surrender. The story that the commander removed his shirt and waved that at the aircraft is strongly disputed by Rahmlow. It also seems highly unlikely that he undressed, especially as he would have been wearing several layers of clothing on top of his shirt. Had he wanted something white, he could have got it quicker by asking for a sheet to be brought up rather than by undressing in an uncomfortably cold and damp wind.

There was insufficient room on the top of the conning tower for the entire crew, so some of the more agile climbed down on to the upper deck, where they opened the storage containers for rubber dinghies. Apparently these were removed without orders and were then washed and blown off the deck before anyone could board them. This left Rahmlow in the unenviable predicament of having no means of evacuating the wounded. Starting the diesel engines was out of the question because of the poisonous gases in the interior and the aircraft would no doubt have attacked the moment it realised the boat was making headway. So, Rahmlow considered himself to have been left with only two options: either to die or to surrender.

He ordered the secrets to be destroyed, the interior to be smashed and for water entry points to be prepared for opening. The plan was to get the wounded off and then follow the Royal Navy to Iceland. Once within sight of land, the men would open the sea cocks, jump overboard and swim ashore. The possibility of the entire crew being removed before the boat got that far does not seem to have occurred to Rahmlow. A day later, he appeared to be completely surprised when the Royal Navy wanted to take him away with the injured men. As a last minute gesture, he tried changing places with the first watch officer, but this was rumbled and he was removed by the boarding party. However, he was assured that the boat would be sunk before reaching land.

The strange point about this last statement is that, according to the engineering officer, when the crew were being taken off, he and some of the men from the technical division were still working below on destroying the interior. Apparently the engineering officer only came to the top of the conning tower after being tricked into doing so by his own men. He did not know exactly how things were going on the outside and, when he climbed up, he believed that the commander wanted to discuss progress with him. Arriving on the bridge, he found himself surrounded by an armed boarding party, who quickly manhandled him out of the way. It is highly unlikely that there was anyone among the British boarding party who could speak German well enough to give the correct order for the engineering officer to come up to the bridge. Therefore this vital instruction must have come from one of *U570's* crew who knew the British had boarded.

Later, shortly after the officers had arrived at Grizedale Hall, a prisoner of war camp in the English Lake District, it became generally known in the camp that *U570* had hoisted a white flag of surrender to an aircraft. The senior prisoner there was Korvkpt Otto Kretschmer of *U99*, who was promoted after the sinking of his boat and who convened the secret court of enquiry which was mentioned earlier. When the men in the prison camp then learned that *U570* was lying at Barrow-in-Furness, only some 40km from Grizedale Hall, Berns volunteered to escape and sink the boat. He was eagerly helped by the colleagues who had earlier ostracised him, but despite being given forged papers, some English money and civilian clothing, he was caught by the Home Guard and shot while running away. The story goes that the Home Guard

Above: This photograph of Italian submariners, taken by the war correspondent Walter Schöppe, was used to illustrate Rahmlow's magazine article during the mid-1950s. Life was not quite as squashed as this might suggest and there was a little more personal space, even in the confines of the crowded bow torpedo room.

shouted three times for him to stop before shooting him in the back. This could well be the case, for in their eagerness to defend the country from invasion, the Home Guard also shot dead more than one British person for every week of the war. This rather sad end of a young life made the British authorities aware of something being afoot and Rahmlow was moved to a camp occupied mainly by army and air force officers, who did not take such a keen interest in the capture of a U-boat.

Now, to look at the same sequence of events from the British point of view. Catalina 'J', piloted by Flying Officer E. A. Jewiss, took over from Hudson 'S' with the instructions to watch the U-boat until darkness. Then, if the Royal Navy had not shown up, the Germans were to be warned to get off before their boat was to be sunk. This almost happened, had it not been for the armed trawler *Northern Chief*, under the command of Lt N. L. Knight, appearing some 12 hours after *U570's* surrender, when it was still light in those northern latitudes. By that time the weather had worsened considerably, making it suicidal to attempt launching a small boat. So, there was nothing more that could be done, other than hope that the next day would bring better conditions. The trawler flashed over a message saying that survivors would not be picked up if the U-boat went down during the night, hoping the harsh words would scare the men into not scuttling the boat.

The waves were still mountainous when the next set of reinforcements arrived. *Northern Chief* was first joined by another armed trawler, the *Kingston Agate* and then by the destroyer *Burwell* and later by two more armed trawlers, *Wastwater* and *Windermere*. This busy conglomeration of small ships was also joined by the

Canadian corvette *Niagara*. At dawn the group was attacked by an aircraft with two depth charges, neither of which caused any significant damage, although the onslaught did cause the men on both sides to hold their breaths. The water was still too rough for rowing boats, but in the end a line was shot across from *Kingston Agate* and Lt H. B. Campbell crossed over in an inflatable dinghy. Some time after this, all of the Germans were taken off and *U570* was towed to Iceland and beached there.

At home in Britain, no one put any great odds on the venture coming off and it was three days later before four submarine experts were flown out to examine *U570*. Lying broadside on to a heavy swell, the boat resembled a stranded whale, leaning over at such a precarious angle that it looked as if it would topple over, but the soft sand offered sufficient support to prevent any last minute catastrophes.

The Royal Navy's description of the inside, written in a confidential military report and therefore without embroidery from an offensive propaganda system, needs to be savoured in full because it gives an excellent insight into why men were so terribly keen on vacating the interior of damaged submarines. Climbing down the ladder, the British experts were greeted with an incredible stench rising out of total darkness. One of the two heads (or lavatories) was being used to store food and, even with the best will in the world, there is no way that one head

could cope with the natural pressure created by about 50 well-fed men. Buckets, used as makeshift conveniences, had spilled not only urine but also a good quantity of faeces into the water, which was lying knee-deep in some places. Dried fruit, beans, peas, quantities of flour, porridge oats and masses of black bread had fallen into the brew to add a most unpleasant quality to an already horrid concoction. And, if this was not enough, a good proportion of vomit from seasick sailors added more stimulating variation to the vile odour.

The Royal Navy men found their immediate task foul, and needed a strong shot of military discipline to perform the task they had been sent to do. However, cleaning up the mess was not their primary objective. There was still the very strong danger of *U570* turning over completely or even sinking into the softness of the sand which was supporting her. Too little compressed air remained in the system to make the boat float properly, though an external compressor, brought over from a corvette, helped in making it lie better in the water. During this initial tour of exploration, the men had no choice other than to wade through the foul mess, but the self-discipline required for the task was worth it. Their survey revealed that it was not so much of a wreck as the Germans had made out. In fact *U570* was in quite reasonable condition, much better than the few smashed instruments suggested at first sight. That stinking heap of German technology had stood up surprisingly well to Squadron Leader Thompson's accurate attack.

Some batteries were cracked, but there was no sign of any chlorine or other dangerous gases. What was more, there was no sign of any such gases having been there at the time of surrender. Breathing gear was not required and it was the stench from the sewage and vomit rather than poisonous gases which was most offensive. The reason why much of the machinery refused to function was simply because a number of fuses and main switches had fallen out. The switches were not damaged and were made to work again by merely setting them back to their 'on' positions. There was an abundance of glass and broken crockery, and in the engine room glass domes over oil intakes were smashed allowing oil to ooze out, but the men could not find anything which would prevent the boat from diving. Even the lack of the electrical power due to the cracked batteries did not present an insuperable problem.

U570 was quickly restored to acceptable seaworthiness and then someone had the job of shovelling out the stinking mess. The Royal Navy report concluded by saying that the lack of serious damage was most surprising, especially as the crew had more than 24 hours before the British boarding party arrived. In view of this, it seemed strange that the interior had not been totally demolished. Even that vital piece of equipment, the deep diving gauge, was found to be functioning. It was only the one used for keeping the boat at periscope depth and the shallow depth gauge which had been blown open by the detonating depth charges.

The examiners suggested that the men of *U570* added to their own demise by allowing a shoddy state of affairs to exist in their boat. It is now impossible to determine whether it was due to negligence, inexperience or sheer idle bloody-mindedness that these slapdash conditions were tolerated. Just to give a few examples of faults: the engines were somewhat out of tune and needed to be reset before they would run smoothly; there were minor defects in several of the auxiliary machines, making them usable but irritating; some electrical connections were not screwed down properly so as to create loose contacts and this resulted in parts of the connectors melting due to the heat generated by sparks in the joint; some exposed metals parts would not run smoothly because they had not been greased. Even worse, U570 had gone to sea with the spare torpedoes not properly stowed. One of them had moved a considerable distance during the depth charge attack to pierce an oil drum and thereby make an unnecessary mess. Despite all this, the Royal Navy found it difficult to understand why the Germans had surrendered their boat. They could only assume that lights going out and the gauges being smashed produced a disgraceful panic.

Whatever the cause, the British learned many useful facts from the incident. They now knew for certain that boats could easily go much deeper than the maximum settings on their depth charges, and much more. In fact they learned virtually all the secrets in the U-boat commander's handbook. This was a terrific help in understanding the significance of decrypted signals and it helped escort commanders to make their attacks more deadly. Above all, the capture of U570 was an excellent consolation for having lost U110 and provided a wealth of propaganda opportunities. This event certainly impressed the British leadership. U570 was one of the few U-boats mentioned by Winston Churchill in his memoirs. Incidentally, it may be of interest to add that a typewriter from U570 is now on display at Bletchley Park.

Although it has often been claimed that U570 was the only U-boat to have surrendered to an aircraft, this is not quite correct because U573 (Kplt Heinrich Heinsohn) surrendered to Hudson 'M' of No 233 Squadron, RAF, piloted by Sergeant Brent on 1 May 1942. Brent straddled the target with two well-placed depth charges and then watched it sink below the surface. When the boat surfaced a short while later, men held up their arms in the air and made no effort to man their anti-aircraft gun. Consequently, Brown did not attack a second time. There were no supporting forces in the area and Hudson 'M' had to leave 30 minutes later due to shortage of fuel. Heinsohn took the opportunity of repairing the severe damage and then making for Spain. Entering the neutral port of Cartagena during the following day, U573 was first interned and then, later, sold to be commissioned into the Spanish Navy as G7.

Following this, Britain issued an order that air crews should not accept surrenders from submarines unless surface forces were in a position to take possession of the prize. One wonders how such an instruction would have been interpreted by the International Tribunal at Nuremberg, had it been given by a German. He would probably have been accused of issuing an order to murder innocent seamen!

It is interesting to add that another boat was heavily hammered by the RAF in the same area where U573 was almost sunk. U595 (Kptlt Jürgen Quaet-Faslem) was so seriously damaged on 14 November 1942 that it was beached near Tenes (Algeria) after a battle lasting for more than an hour. During that time, the crew took the opportunity of throwing secret documents and the Enigma machine overboard.

Below: U570 in her new identity as HMS Graph, flying the White Ensign of the Royal Navy.

Chapter 8
Shark — The Four-wheel Enigma Code

Boarding U559

In February 1942, nine months after the secret capture of *U110*, the U-boat arm changed its cipher system by introducing a fourth wheel for the Enigma machine. This was done quite simply by providing thinner wheels, some with the original wiring, so that four could fit into the slot previously occupied by three. Sadly for the men who served in U-boats, this was done at a time when other radical changes were taking place in the general pattern of the war which meant that no one in Germany noticed the diminished effectiveness of British intelligence. This single omission must rank as one of the biggest blunders of the war.

Above: *U559* with partly extended sky or navigation periscope. The commander's flag pole on the left of the periscope was usually removed when the boat went to

The most significant change in the Atlantic was created by America's entry into the war. Deserting the difficult mid-ocean, U-boats found the Americans reluctant even to take the most basic precautions to prevent their merchant marine from being decimated off their own coast. Consequently, sinkings rose to an all-time high, often called the 'Second Happy Time', but this state of affairs did not last long. Six months later, by the summer of 1942, larger, long-distance boats were forced south into the Caribbean, while smaller ones returned to the harshness of mid-Atlantic. There they soon realised that the 'Air-Gap' was becoming narrower and escorts were noticeably more ferocious. The winning of their daily bread was not only becoming more difficult, but also increasingly more precarious.

On the other side, Britain and the United States were not yet assured of victory in the Atlantic. Indeed, the autumn of 1942 was one of the most depressing periods for the Allies. In August, the daily average number of U-boats in the Atlantic had reached 100 and remained at that all-time high until the late spring of the following year. Britain, however, had made fantastic progress with its anti-U-boat campaign, introducing more effective techniques, a greater number of ships and aircraft, and by making use of new technology. The success of individual U-boats had therefore diminished considerably but the appearance of such vast numbers meant that merchant shipping losses remained relatively high. To beat this giant conundrum, the Allies desperately needed an insight into Triton, the new four-wheel Enigma code being used by U-boats. Britain had appropriately named this new code 'Shark'.

The breakthrough came quite unexpectedly in the autumn of 1942, when men from the Royal Navy boarded *U559* in the far eastern Mediterranean, capturing material which enabled Bletchley Park to get back into the U-boat code and from then read the Enigma messages for the Atlantic. Neither the boat nor the commander is terribly well known and hardly feature in any of the early histories of the war. Yet, Kptlt Hans Heidtmann was a Knight of the Iron Cross, suggesting he contributed more than most to the sea battles. *U559* sailed for her first operational war cruise on 4 June 1941, shortly after the capture of *U110* and the sinking of the battleship *Bismarck*, but before the surrender of *U570*. During her

first cruise, the crew saw the ferocity of thc North Atlantic, experiencing the severity of the weather as well as the frustration caused by hunting elusive convoys. In addition to this, they suffered punishment from aggressive escorts. Despite these hardships, U559 did not come home empty handed. Later, in September 1941, Heidtmann became one of six commanders who were ordered to form a first wave of U-boats to be sent into the Mediterranean. Passing through the Strait of Gibraltar, he arrived in Salamis (Greece, near Athens) on 20 October, exactly one month after having left St Nazaire. U559 continued to participate in the thick of the action, although it would appear that Heidtmann's contribution was not fully recognised at the time. He was not awarded his Knight's Cross until much later, when he had already been a prisoner of war for five months.

Heidtmann was born in a country railway station near Lübeck on 8 August 1914, less than two weeks after the outbreak of World War 1. At the age of 20, he joined the navy as an officer candidate and then gained experience in a variety of surface ships before enduring his submarine training. At the beginning of World War 2, he was first watch officer in U33, the boat which later went down in the Clyde estuary and supplied Britain with the first Enigma wheels. Heidtmann left U33 after the end of her first war voyage to become an apprentice commander in U14 under Herbert Wohlfarth.

Heidtmann was an unpretentious, quiet person, well liked by his men and respected for his calm professional-ism. It was on 29 September 1942, one year and nine days after having arrived in the Mediterranean, that he set out from Messina in Sicily for his last war cruise. He certainly was not the complacent type nor the highly aggressive hero who had to have a go at everything at any cost. When the end finally came, he was well prepared and made a great effort to get his men out of their boat before it entombed them. Much of U559's story seems to round off with coincidences and easy numbers. Even her end came almost exactly one month after leaving Messina. It was shortly after sunrise on 30 October 1942 that a Sunderland, flying on general maritime reconnaissance, made contact with something resembling a submarine. Unfortunately for the airmen, the crystal clear Mediterranean morning also assured that alert lookouts on the conning tower spotted the flying giant. The contact on the radar screen vanished long before the Sunderland reached the spot and a closer examination of the empty sea revealed nothing but calm, blue water.

The airmen were left wondering whether there had been anything in the water at all. Had that blip on the radar screen been an illusion or a reflection from the surface of the sea? Such mistakes had been made before and now more than one man watched the screen when anything out of the ordinary appeared. This seemed to confirm that the echo had definitely been there. It had to be

Above: Kptlt Hans (Johannes) Heidtmann with white cap cover on the bridge of *U559*. Around the beginning of the war it became a fad for commanders to be the only ones to wear a white cap on board. Some authors have suggested that this was an order from the Naval High Command to make it easier for men to recognise authority, which is not true. Submariners lived so close together that each man knew everyone on board so well this would be completely unnecessary.

Above: U559 in the Mediterranean with a bucket dredger in the background. Docking was a tricky manoeuvre and piers with special fenders were often provided to prevent the underwater hydroplanes from being buckled.

Above: Men lining up on the upper deck of *U559* in the Mediterranean. The two jumping wires over their heads would suggest that they are standing on the after deck.

a submarine. However, it was not until the news was reported back to base that people could be totally certain that it was not British. They were close to Port Said in Egypt, the northern end of the Suez Canal and hub of British naval activity, meaning the Sunderland could well have caught one of its own boats. The blunder of attacking one's own side had been made before. HMS *Oxley*, the first British submarine to be sunk during the war, went down as a result of a torpedo fired from HMS *Triton*. What is more, Britain did not have exclusivity in this field. German units were also responsible for sinking a good number of their own ships.

As luck would have it, the destroyer HMS *Hero* (Lt-Cdr W. Scott) arrived within the hour after intercepting the call from the Sunderland, so that both ship and aircraft continued the search, but nothing was found, not even with the aid of Asdic. It was around midday when four more ships, the destroyers *Pakenham* (Capt E. K. B. Stevens), *Petard* (Lt-Cdr Mark Thornton), *Dulverton* (Cdr W. N. Petch) and *Hurworth* (Lt D. A. Shaw) appeared from Port Said, with the support of a Wellesley bomber from No 47 Squadron, RAF. *Pakenham* had been sweeping the area with Asdic for less than an hour when the positive 'pong' from a submerged object was heard. By this time tactics had changed considerably and she no longer put on a spurt of speed to drop depth charges with the vague hope of hitting the target, the reason being that Asdic contact was lost once the hunter came too close and therefore drop depth charges had to be dropped 'blind'. Although the time between losing contact and dropping charges was not terribly long, it did give the U-boat commander the edge by allowing him to speed up

and change direction to move out of the way of the blast. After all, he could hear the Asdic pings as well as the propeller noises and the splashes of depth charges hitting the water. Calling up *Petard*, *Pakenham* kept the submerged boat in Asdic contact while her consort manoeuvred on top to drop a set of five charges, adjusted to a variety of depths. This did not produce any results, other than disturb the men in *U559*. They had been through this before. Frightening as it may have been, they knew that the old man could outmanoeuvre anyone on the surface. What was more, the blast from the explosions created such a chaotic disturbance in the water that it took a while for things to settle down and for Asdic to regain contact. Inside the U-boat, the situation was uncomfortable and frightening, but not necessarily life-threatening.

The second time, with the U-boat now held in cross bearings from two Asdic sets, more depth charges were dropped by a third ship. Once again nothing much happened. The cat and mouse game continued with the surface ships losing contact, regaining it, homing in with the haunting sound of Asdic and then plastering the area with more depth charges. Every time nothing. Just deafening blasts. More depth charges. More blasts, but no results. Lunch had long been forgotten. That blasted Asdic set had put paid to a restful meal. Now it was starting to get dark and there were still no results. This was the sort of infuriating moment when sailors started questioning the sanity of their commanding officers. Was he just chasing a shoal of fish? Or a layer of cold water

down in the depths? Both were possible. Why on earth did the officers have to slog on when everybody could see there was nothing there?

It was not only the cursing men on deck who questioned the sanity of the commanding officers. During such prolonged hunts, escort captains themselves often started wondering whether there was any point in going on. Yet, despite the frustration, determination dictated that the hunt should continue. Someone even came up with the novel idea that the submarine might be deeper than the maximum setting of the depth charges and suggested plugging the holes of the primer with soap. Anything was worth a try, but at first it did not seem to make much difference, other than lengthen the time between depth charges being launched and them exploding.

At the receiving end, things had been uncomfortable for some time. Heidtmann had passed beyond the stage where every commander wished the next depth charge would put an end to the misery. Having been down so long meant the interior of the boat smelt like a public lavatory which had not been cleaned for a long time. Most of the crew had retired to their bunks with breathing gear. For those who had work to do absolute silence was the order of the day. If they had to walk about they even wrapped their shoes with rags to prevent any possible scraping or clanking.

Although none of the exploding depth charges had been fatal, they did create considerable havoc. Glass in gauges smashed. Lights often went out. Men stumbled along with the aid of stark torch beams. Things were upset. Water squirted in. Machinery had to be repaired.

One incident followed another, but the all-important deep diving gauge remained intact, making it possible to keep the boat deep down in the cellar where the incredibly high water pressure ensured that detonations would be least effective, the blast influencing a smaller area. Nothing was critical. Nothing was fatal. *U559* survived. In the end it was the intensity of the long hunt which brought the boat to the surface. The foul air in the submarine would have held for the best part of another day, but the constant spurts of high speed to get away from the depth charges were taking their toll. The men in *U559* had counted 288 of them and most were close enough to make everybody think that the next was going to kill.

This extra consumption of power was draining the batteries and the electricity was essential for maintaining depth. This critical point, combined with the extra deep set depth charges finally forced *U559* to the surface. Knowing that he could not survive any longer, Heidtmann prepared to abandon ship as quickly as possible. So, it was a case of opening sea vents and surfacing while everybody clambered out exceedingly fast. This was a manoeuvre nobody ever practised. It was also virtually impossible to get the timing exactly right. No one could know how long it would take for the interior to fill with water and sink. Yet, almost fifty lives depended on the boat not going down too fast.

On the surface, men aboard HMS *Petard* were just as worn out as those in the submarine. They had been on the go for over 12 hours, suffering in the intense heat of an unforgiving sun. Much of that time was spent at action stations, which did not allow them to rest. It was during the cool evening, at 2240 hours, when they caught the distinctive stench of diesel oil and almost instantly the Asdic operator reported the characteristic hiss of compressed air being blown into diving tanks. A white patch started appearing on the black surface of the water shortly before the submarine sloshed to the surface. A searchlight beam framed the conning tower while *Petard*'s 4in gun and a number of smaller calibres opened fire. Things were starting to happen quickly, much faster than it takes to write or even read. At first the Royal Navy was intent on sinking the quarry, but amidst the excited confusion it was realised that a boarding party might get on board. The staccato gunfire of the night turned into a frightening stillness where the blackness, cut by that brilliant white beam, was punctuated only by the lapping of water against metal and by the cries of men as the crew of *U559* abandoned ship.

Sub-Lt Gordon Connel launched the whaler, while the first lieutenant, Antony Fasson and Able Seaman Colin Grazier stripped off to swim over to the U-boat. They were joined by 16-year-old canteen assistant Tommy Brown, who had lied about his age in order to get into the navy. *U559* had at least one 4in hole in her, plus several dozen smaller hits, and now looked almost ghostly in the brilliantly stark beam of the searchlight. The Royal Navy's planners had given thought to the possibility of boarding a U-boat for some time and Fasson therefore knew what he was looking for. The majority of ships which might come into contact with a U-boat had specially prepared men on board. Instantly, without taking time to calculate the risk, Fasson and Grazier climbed down inside, smashed locked cupboard doors and handed vital parts to Brown, who made three trips up to the top of the conning tower, carefully carrying those items handed to him. Another seaman, Ken Lacroix helped by lowering a rope to haul up some of the heavier items. Everything was carefully stowed aboard the whaler when Brown realised the boat was sinking. He shouted for the other two to come up, but although they were now standing in two feet of rising water, they handed him another pile and continued their search. Suddenly, without warning, as he reached the top of the ladder, the boat slipped deeper. Brown shouted down into the dim stench. This time the two men below responded to his cry, but water rushed down the open hatch before they could escape. Brown cleared the conning tower, gasping for air when he realised it was all over. Connel and some other men were washed off, but the U-boat sank with Fasson and Grazier still on board.

Their sacrifice had been more than incredible. It enabled Bletchley Park to get back into the U-boat code and gave the cryptanalysts a number of essential code books to help understand the torrent of Enigma messages constantly flowing in. The bravery of the three men did not qualify for a Victoria Cross because their action had not been in the face of an enemy, so they were awarded the George Cross instead. Sadly, Tommy Brown, the youngest person ever to receive the medal, died before it was awarded. Two months before the end of the war, while he was serving as a senior canteen assistant aboard the cruiser HMS *Belfast*, the ship put in for a refit in Tynemouth, where Tommy's family lived, and he was given permission to sleep at home. He died there in a tragic house fire. Heidtmann and the majority of his men survived to become prisoners of war. Despite the intense gunfire, only seven men lost their lives.

The Dive

Today an abundance of excellent reference books makes the reconstruction of historical events relatively easy, but even as recently as the early 1980s it was a totally different matter. Until the 1970s the British establishment considered much of the U-boat war to be top secret and finding the truth was often exceedingly difficult Some research was made more arduous by events such as three U-boats sinking in exactly the same position and similar names appearing under similar circumstances, but at different times. One of these fascinating confusions, hovering over the sinking of *U559*, came to light some 12 years after the war when Peter Keeble, a Royal Navy commander, published the book *Ordeal by Water*. In it he describes how he had dived in the Mediterranean on the wreck of '*U307*'.

The fact that a person of such standing should get the number wrong, especially as he was so closely involved, sounds absurd today and even in those days it was difficult to grasp. Soon after his book appeared it became apparent that Keeble could not have dived on *U307*

Above: The conning tower of *U205* with Kptlt Friedrich Bürgel on the right. The head lens of the partly raised attack periscope is in the middle and the rod aerial has been extended on the right.

because the boat had never been in the Mediterranean and certainly was not sunk in 1942. *U307* left Harstad in Norway on 17 April 1945 under the command of ObltzS Erich Krüger and was depth charged by HMS *Loch Insh* off the north of Norway at the end of that month.

To make matters worse, Keeble did not give an exact date for his dive, but it is possible to reconstruct the approximate time from events which he describes. This places the dive a short time after the sinking of *U559*, making Heidtmann's boat the most likely candidate. Collecting facts produced powerful evidence that Keeble had indeed dived on *U559*. There were certainly a large number of similarities between his description and this boat:

1. The location was in the eastern Mediterranean near Port Said.

2. An aircraft first made radar contact and then a P-Class destroyer arrived for an Asdic search.

3. A submerged boat was brought to the surface by depth charges.

4. The U-boat surrendered.

5. The surrender took place at night.

6. The boat remained afloat long enough for a British boarding party to get on board.

7. The boat sank with Royal Navy boarders on board.

8. Important documents were salvaged from the U-boat.

9. A P-Class destroyer, HMS *Paladin*, was involved.

Paladin, *Petard*, *Pakenham*? Did someone get the names wrong? Seeing the words side by side, it is obvious that they are different, but chasing after information in the Imperial War Museum in London, at the Royal Navy's Submarine Museum in Gosport near Portsmouth, the Bundesarchiv in Germany and other far-flung locations did produce some doubt. Could they be talking about the same ship?

The decisive step came after a close examination of a chart revealed that *U559* sank in deep water, water far too deep for a diver. So, it could not have been *U559* after all. But *Paladin*, what had she to do with the story? She had sunk an Italian submarine in the Mediterranean. Was this what records were referring to? Naval records published immediately after the war suggested that she did sink a U-boat in the eastern Mediterranean on 17 February 1943, just a few months after the *U559* incident. Some 20 boats disappeared around that period, but finding one on operations close to Port Said was not easy. It must be borne in mind that the majority of researchers had to rely on a variety of documents strewn about in widely separated archives. There were hardly any accurate lists nor a great many reference books.

Finally, it appeared that *U205* under Kptlt Friedrich Bürgel fitted the description. Having got a positive identification, it was becoming easier to piece together Keeble's heroic dive. The idea of him having been a charlatan with a fertile imagination had crossed the minds of several people, yet this seemed unlikely. The reason for so many shortcomings in his book and his economical use of the facts appears more likely to have been due to him steering too close to the British Official Secrets Act. In 1957, when he published his book, the Act would still have been a severely restricting influence on authors like Keeble. The severity with which the establishment attempted to curtail knowledge of the war in those days can hardly be imagined today and the reasons for wanting to keep the events of the war under a tight cloak of secrecy are difficult to comprehend, but this was a fact of life for many years after the end of the hostilities.

Further investigation into the activities of *U205* has produced a jumble of contradicting figures and facts. The following appears to be the most likely sequence of

Above: U205 with commander's flag pole in position next to the circular radio direction finder aerial. The large circular feature under the coat of arms of the City of Salzburg is the radio aerial intake. The thin wire connecting this with the thick jumping wire can hardly be seen.

Above: Success pennants aboard *U205* being supported by the partly raised attack periscope. Some boats wrote the tonnage of the sunk ships on the flags, others added the name and sometimes the men used the boat's unofficial emblem.

events, although anyone turning up new documents could well find that there are some errors in this brief account. It seems likely that she left Salamis in Greece on 2 February 1943, attacked a convoy some 100km northwest of Port Said on the 7th and then remained in the area for the next 10 days. On the 17th she was spotted and attacked by an aircraft from No 15 Squadron, South African Air Force. Intercepting the sighting report, the destroyer *Paladin* arrived shortly afterwards to help with an Asdic search. Eventually, the boat was brought to the surface by depth charges during the following night and a sharp burst of gunfire encouraged the crew to abandon ship exceedingly quickly. A boarding party succeeded in getting on board to try to salvage documents and other secrets, while the corvette *Gloxinia* attached a tow cable. Although in a precarious state, it looked as if the submarine could be beached on the North African coast. Unfortunately, it went down in deep water, about a kilometre from land and it is highly likely that *U205* was the target of Peter Keeble's momentous dive.

Left: Kptlt Friedrich Bürgel and his men parading on the upper deck of *U205*. The clean appearance of the men would suggest that they are on their way out rather than coming home from a voyage.

Right: Men from *U205* as prisoners of war in Canada. Some men were released soon after the cessation of hostilities, but many remained in British and American hands for another 2–3 years after the war, while prisoners in Russia were kept even longer and harshly treated.

Chapter 9
Stranded in Africa

Two U-boats became semi-permanent attachments to the African continent: *U617* under Albrecht Brandi was beached on 12 September 1943 in neutral Spanish Morocco and *U852* under Heinz-Wilhelm Eck in May 1944 near Ras Mabber in the former Italian Somaliland. In both cases the boats were run aground by their own crews after having sustained substantial damage which made it impossible for them to reach a friendly port. The wreck of *U617*, lying within the three-mile limit of a neutral country, was pounded by gunfire from the corvette HMS *Hyacinth* (Cdr R. T. White), the sloop HMAS *Woolongong* (Lt T. H. Smith) and the armed trawler HMS *Haarlem*, but no attempt seems to have been made to board it. The Australian and British ships made a point of remaining outside the territorial limits, but felt justified in bombarding the wreck to assure that it could not be made seaworthy again. Although some have suggested it, there is no reason to believe that any Allied personnel boarded the U-boat to try to find secret material.

Shortly before this, *U617* was one of the few U-boats to have been attacked with a phosphorous bomb. The canister hit the forward edge of the conning tower, from where it showered its fiendish contents over men sheltering from a hail of bullets behind whatever protection the bridge could provide. Phosphorous bombs were rarely used at sea because the substance only burst into flames when exposed to the air. They were used in air raids on civilian targets on land, where they often caused horrendous injuries. The men on the bridge of *U617* were lucky to have been showered by relatively small fragments, meaning their injuries were not life-threatening.

U852, a Type IXD2, had been developed from the earlier long-range Type IXC by adding two further sections, one forward and the other aft of the conning tower. This provided additional crew accommodation as well as space for another set of engines for more efficient cruising. The fuel capacity in the external tanks was greatly enlarged to give the boats an incredibly long range of about 32,000 nautical miles or 60,000km. A standard Type IXC could cover only half that distance and a Type VIIC, like *U617*, less than a third.

The modification also presented a large number of disadvantages, which made the boats unsuitable for the all-out convoy war in the Atlantic. Hydroplanes were not enlarged, which tended to make the boats behave like floundering whales, making it difficult to control them while diving. Even worse, it was virtually impossible to keep them at periscope depth without the bows or stern sometimes breaking through the surface of the water.

Above: Korvkpt Albrecht Brandi, commander of *U617*, on the right, and Konteradmiral Leo Kreisch (Flag Officer for U-boats in Italy). Brandi was one of only two U-boat men who were awarded the Knight's Cross with Oakleaves, Swords and Diamonds. A partly raised attack periscope with the small head lens can be seen holding up flags in the background.

This problem might have been rectified by longer periscopes, but such devices would have taken some time to develop and the builders were forced into using optical equipment already available.

The South Atlantic and Indian Ocean coasts of Africa tend to conjure up idyllic visions of remote beaches, but already the first U-boat to operate there (*U178* under KptzS Hans Ibbeken) during the autumn of 1942 had found the going unexpectedly hard. The reason being that *U178* sailed into a legacy left by the 'ghost cruisers' or surface raiders of earlier times. These had caused such fear and disruption that considerable steps were taken to assure the safety of the sea lanes and to maintain far-off support for the Allied war effort. *U178*, for example, found an unusually high proportion of targets being escorted by aircraft and an abundant use of radar, making attacks risky undertakings. In addition to this, it was soon discovered that the southern seas were either too stormy for the employment of weapons or the mirror smooth surface made it easy for aircraft to spot anything which left bow waves. Aircraft were more than a real pain. They presented incredible opposition. The other drawback, as far as the Germans were concerned, was that there was relatively little radio traffic, making it easy for the enemy to identify and track them.

During his briefing for *U852's* forthcoming voyage into the Indian Ocean and then on to Penang in Malaya, Eck was warned about the intensity of air cover and the need to distance himself from any incriminating evidence left on the surface after sinking ships. This fear of driving a slow, vulnerable boat through such powerful opposition persuaded him to machine-gun the floating wreckage and thereby the survivors from the freighter SS *Peleus* which he had sunk off West Africa during the afternoon of 13 March 1944. After the war Eck was tried for war crimes. He became the only U-boat commander to be sentenced to death by an Allied court. An interesting point about this trial is that it was delayed until after the war, when there was no danger of the Germans executing Allied prisoners who had carried out similar acts. Indeed, accusations of German and Japanese survivors being killed have not even been investigated.

Survivors from the *Peleus* were landed towards the end of April 1944, having been rescued by the Polish freighter *Alexandre Silva*. In addition to this, survivors from *U852's* second victim (the 5277-ton British freighter *Dahomian*, which went down within sight of Cape Point [South Africa] on 1 April 1944) were rescued a few days later. This information, together with an analysis of radio signals, made it possible to guess where *U852* was going. Adding the estimated speed to this formula, the RAF started sending out air patrols as soon as the boat was within range of the British base in Aden. These efforts paid dividends on 2 May 1944. *U852* was sighted on its 105th day at sea. The length of such a voyage was an incredible achievement in itself. The boat was unbearably hot, with a high proportion of the men suffering from home- and sea-sickness in the confinement of their cramped quarters where they could see neither sky nor sun. Not having seen action for some time probably lulled the men into a false sense of security and this, combined with an almost total lack of exercise, induced an unrecognised lethargy. Yet, despite this drawback, August Hoffmann, the second watch officer on duty with the lookouts, reacted with calculated calm when he ordered *U852* into an emergency dive.

The tell-tale V-shaped bow wave on the surface of an almost fluorescent sea had already been spotted by men in Wellington 'E', piloted by Flying Officer H.R. Mitchell, who had made the most of his advantage by manoeuvring between the glaring sun and his tiny target. Then, going down with the greatest of determination, he sprayed the boat with everything his aircraft could shoot and, at the same time, straddled it with a number of well-placed

Below: U617 shortly after running aground in North Africa.

depth charges. *U852* was on the way down by the time these exploded and, when Mitchell regained height, he found the seas empty and calm, almost as if nothing had happened. Only the increasing concentric rings from the dying eruption indicated that there had been an act of aggression. Unfortunately there was not much else he could do. His fuel was running low and this dictated an immediate return to base. Still stunned, the men in *U852* fumbled for their personal respirators as choking fumes filled the boat, indicating that acid was leaking out of the batteries and mixing with seawater in the bilges. Despite the incredible hammering, the technical division's 15-minute-long struggle eventually brought the boat back to the surface. The damage assessment indicated that another dive would certainly be the last. So Eck was left with only one option: to get out of the area fast, but doing this on the surface under the midday sun meant he had to count on more attacks before darkness offered him some hope of a respite.

There were more aircraft attacks during the day, but *U852*'s gunners put up a terrific show while the boat tried twisting away from death. The final blow was struck early on 3 May by Flying Officer J. R. Forrester, flying another Wellington. However, by this time he could also see the jagged Somali coast ahead of the U-boat, making it plain that Eck was hoping to get ashore before his boat was sunk. The blood and flesh spluttered around from seven men killed as a result of gunfire had sickened a good proportion of the crew, yet they struggled on with resolute determination to survive and to destroy their boat. Once grounded close to a rugged shore, the boat was left in peace for the men to make the best out of their pernicious situation. They knew that they were close to Ras Mabber in the former Italian Somaliland, but that Italian colony had been occupied by the Allies since 1941. Yet the men were pleased to be alive on dry land and offered no resistance when they were rounded up by Somali Camel Corps troops, supported by a landing party from HMS *Falmouth*. The Royal Navy dispatched a boarding party to the U-boat where a few interesting items, including the boat's log with the exact details of the sinking of the *Peleus*, were picked up. Apparently the investigation of the wreck was so thorough that engineers even drilled holes in the pressure hull to measure its thickness.

The U-boat Command was aware of what had happened, which would suggest that details of the proposed beaching were radioed to base and it seems likely that the men then carried out the stan-dard procedure of discarding the Enigma machine and its codes as well as other secret material. In the event of such drastic action being a false alarm and them needing to make further transmissions, a special emergency cipher pad was carried for such exceedingly rare occurrences. Although the crew had ample time for the destruction of secrets, one wonders whether injuries might have prevented them from making a thorough job of the process. The vicious air attacks had killed seven men while their boat struggled to cover a distance of over 200km. The all-important log book was left for the Royal Navy to pick up, so it could well be that other sensitive documents also passed into Allied hands.

Below: U852 after having been run aground in Somalia. This long-range boat of Type IXD2 was on its way to the Far East when it was attacked by aircraft and seriously damaged.

Below: Men from the Royal Navy inspecting the wreck of *U852* after it had been beached in Somalia.

Chapter 10
The Capture of *U505*

For long before its capture *U505* had been suffering an almost incredible run of bad luck and misfortune. This can perhaps be said to have begun in June 1942 in the Caribbean when the then commander Axel-Olaf Loewe had his first war cruise as captain brought to a rather dramatic end when he fell ill. He requested permission to return home. Once back in France, he immediately went into hospital to have an inflamed appendix removed and had not recovered sufficiently by the time the boat was ready for sea again, therefore 24-year-old Peter Zschech took over command. Things looked quite good at first. He had learned his trade in *U124* under Johann Mohr and began with success just like Loewe before his illness, but this spell of good fortune did not last long. Back in the Caribbean, three days after sinking a large freighter, *U505* was almost totally demolished during an accurate attack by a Hudson aircraft piloted by Flight Sergeant Sillcock. The blast wrecked the entire aft section of the upper deck, turning it into a tangled web of twisted iron and even set off the loaded 37mm gun. The greatest of efforts were required to save lives and to keep the boat afloat. Unable to dive, *U505* was instantly converted into a sitting duck with grim prospects of ever reaching land again. Luckily some relief was close at hand. Another frontline boat, *U68* under Karl-Friedrich Merten, provided vital spare parts and *U462*, a purpose-built supply boat under the command of Bruno Vowe, brought a doctor, together with a plentiful supply of morphine to relieve the suffering of several wounded men.

Although still a wreck with only limited diving restored, *U505* succeeded in crawling back to France, where the bad luck continued. After seven months in dock for repairs the usual deep diving trials, during the early stages of the next outward-bound passage, revealed a few minor problems which could not be repaired on board. Zschech had no alternative other than to return to Lorient. Every one of the next four missions had to be broken off as well shortly after setting out, due to hidden mechanical faults of one kind or another. This was not only frustrating for the men in *U505*, but also forced the dockyard commander to examine the procedures under which repair gangs worked. Some of the French labourers were found guilty of sabotage and sentenced to death by firing squad.

The following voyage, starting on 9 October 1943, also ran into problems. Two weeks after leaving Lorient, *U505* came under a devastating depth charge attack from surface ships. Zschech reacted by withdrawing into his 'cabin' and shooting himself. Paul Meyer, the first watch

officer, who had been with *U505* for 10 months but had never been to sea for a prolonged period, took control. He could hardly continue with the mission because the commander was the only person trained in the intricate art of attacking. In a way it seems strange that only one man on board should know how this had to be carried out. This problem of the first officer not being trained to replace the commander had an even worse consequence for *U415*, which is mentioned in a later chapter.

Harald Lange, the new commander, an officer from the reserve, arrived during a chilly, dull November day while the boat was again lying in Lorient. He had been born on 23 December 1903, making him much older even than Loewe, who at the age of 33 had already been regarded as the 'old man' of the outfit. The fact that, at his age, Lange only held the rank of Oberleutnant-zur-See would suggest that he did not have a great deal of experience. He had served in *Sperrbrecher* (barrier breakers) and in

Above: Axel-Olaf Loewe who commissioned *U505* in August 1941 and then commanded the boat for one year until he became a consultant with U-boat arm's Operations Department.

converted trawler-type patrol boats. But whatever Lange lacked in rank or experience in submarines, he made up with his jovial and precise character. Being a comfortable type, he quickly gained the trust of the men.

His first voyage was brought to an abrupt halt by a distress call and then by a plea, rather than an order, from the Supreme Naval Command for anyone in the area to pick up survivors from a surface action at sea. This event has hardly been recorded in history books, yet it turned into one of the most emotional happenings of the war. The sequence of events started with the 8th Destroyer Flotilla and the 4th Torpedo Boat Flotilla setting out to escort the blockade runner and supply ship *Alsterufer* (Kapitän Piatek) back through the dangerous Bay of Biscay. Unfortunately for the Germans, Bletchley Park could understand enough of the relevant German radio codes to dispatch a more powerful force of cruisers to bring these to battle. *Alsterufer* was first sighted by a Sunderland and then sunk with rockets

from a Liberator. Following this, 74 men in four lifeboats were picked up by Canadian corvettes sent out to rescue them. Next, as luck continued to play into the Allied hands, the German destroyers and torpedo boats ran into the intercepting forces at a time when the weather worsened considerably, meaning the smaller German ships could not use their higher speed to evade the guns of more powerful opponents. Consequently two torpedo boats and one destroyer were sunk, while others sustained considerable damage with significant loss of life.

The distress call was picked up by both *U505* and *U618*, under Kurt Baberg, who also heard the rumble of the guns but was in no position to help. Limping home with severe damage, his boat had been battered into submission while trying to break through the Strait of Gibraltar. It was hardly capable of diving, much of the machinery including the radio transmitter did not work any more, and many of the crew were injured. Knowing that his boat would not withstand further contact with the opposition, Baberg was more than reluctant to change course, but he also felt he could not leave colleagues to die at sea. Not knowing what he should do, and not wanting

Above: This insignificant looking photograph was taken during a momentous occasion in history when *U180* met the Japanese submarine *I-29* in the Indian Ocean to transfer two passengers from Europe, the Indian Nationalist Subhas Chandra Bose and the Arab Abid Hasan. The man in the dinghy, smoking a cigarette, is Harald Lange, who later commanded *U180* and then went on to become commander of *U505*. He is obviously doing something unconventional, but hasn't discarded his hat.

Right: Harald Lange as commander of *U505*.

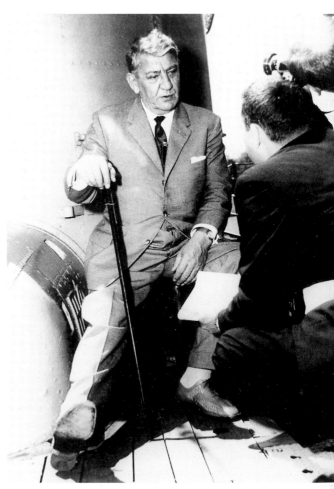

Above: Harald Lange being photographed long after the war on the deck of *U505* at the Science and Industry Museum in Chicago.

to burden his battered crew with another seemingly impossible task, he put the matter to the vote, something virtually unheard of in a U-boat. To his surprise there was not a single voice against the proposition. So, the battered wreck changed course, to be rewarded with finding 25 survivors from the destroyer *Z27*.

U505 was slightly better off, inasmuch as the boat had not been damaged. Finding 34 survivors from *T25* made the deviation and curtailment of the cruise worth while, but putting into Brest on 2 January 1944, two days before *U618* arrived in Lorient, *U505* experienced another of those frustrating incidents of bad luck. Four months earlier the main ballast pump had forced a return to port and now one of the main electric motors developed a similar fault, burning out in a most dramatic manner. The fire was dealt with by the technical division and was not dangerous so close to harbour. The main problem was that these motors were installed before the boat was built around them. They were bigger than the hatches and could not be got out of or into a boat without drastic action. There was no choice. *U505* had to go into dock for a prolonged period. There, a huge hole was cut in the pressure hull and in the tanks surrounding it, and then, afterwards, everything had to be welded back in place. This was a costly and long undertaking, but gave the crew the opportunity for an unscheduled leave and it was the middle of March 1944 before the boat left for its final war cruise.

The events leading up to the capture of *U505* are best described by the commander, Harald Lange, in an interrogation report he made aboard the aircraft carrier USS *Guadalcanal*. It was around midday of 4 June 1944, two days before the Normandy landings, when the radio operator reported faint propeller noises becoming louder. Focusing on the hardly audible sounds, it quickly became evident that there was more than one source, and the high-pitched whine of warship engines, rather than the characteristic thumping of merchant ships, suggested *U505* was being locked into an unpromising position. Bringing the boat up to periscope depth, Lange made out three destroyers and something much bigger behind them. He also caught sight of a small, single-engine plane, suggesting the huge hulk in the far distance was an aircraft carrier. He did not dare risk examining the scene for too long.

There was little choice. Surfacing would have been suicidal. The only practical course of action was to go deep, but the ghostly ping of Asdic echoing through the boat told everybody that they had already been located. Two tremendous detonations helped *U505* on her descent to a safer depth. Lights went out. Water cascaded into the interior in several places. Much of the electrical machinery, including the all-important ballast pump for expelling the intruding water, refused to function. The rudders jammed. Men were moaning in pain while others were stunned into silence. Those left conscious dealt with the emergencies. Unable to assess the damage or do much about repairing it, it was a case of either dropping down into the depths where water pressure would crush the boat or using the last straw remedy of blowing the diving tanks with compressed air. Lange gave the order for the latter life-saving course of action. Everyone on board knew that this was most likely to result in the boat having to be abandoned.

On the boat breaking surface, Lange was ready waiting by the hatch. Jumping out on to the bridge, he was greeted by a hail of gunfire and the order to abandon ship left his mouth seconds before he lost consciousness. His brain was spinning in painful confusion while blood dripping down his forehead blotted his vision. Regaining some control of his body, he ordered the bows to be turned towards the main source of gunfire so that the men could escape from the back of the conning tower. Soon Lange was surrounded by clambering legs and with blood still obscuring his vision he lost consciousness again. Lange could not judge for how long he lay there.

Next he became aware of being on the upper deck, and tried pulling himself along, but found his body no longer responded to his brain's commands. He had no idea how he got down from the top of the tower and could only lie in semi-consciousness, watching his men release the life-rafts from their pressure-resisting containers. Soon after this, he was washed off the deck, but was lucky enough that a couple of men pulled and pushed him into a life-raft. His life-jacket, like the rest of his body, had been repeatedly punctured by shrapnel and was no longer of any use. The injuries made even simple watching difficult. Later, a large wooden splinter was found to have penetrated his eyelid, narrowly missing the eye itself. He was lucky to be picked up by a destroyer and given the appropriate medical attention. After this, he was transferred to the aircraft carrier where he was told that his boat had been captured.

U505's captors, a Hunter-Killer Group consisting of the aircraft carrier *Guadalcanal* with the destroyers

Below: The rear torpedo compartment of *U505* with the typically blue and white squared naval bed linen. The navy also used such a distinctive pattern on tablecloths, the idea being that it would easily be spotted if stolen. The emergency steering wheel in front of the two torpedo tubes hinged at the top and would usually have been pushed sideways, out of the way.

Chatelain, Flaherty, Jenks, Pillsbury and *Pope,* under the command of Captain Daniel V. Gallery, had sailed from Norfolk, Virginia. Their aim was to concentrate on an area to the south of the Canary Islands, where U-boats were known to congregate for refuelling. The possibility of capturing a U-boat had occurred to Gallery and others, and each ship had formed a specially trained boarding party for that purpose. When *Chatelain* made contact with *U505,* they were some 150 miles from Africa.

As Lange described in his account, the attack was fast and accurate. In fact the first depth charges were thrown so quickly that they could not be adjusted shallow enough. Two Wildcat fighters were quickly sent up to help locate the submerged boat. One of them dived, shooting at the water where the shadow of the boat could be seen. Almost instantly, another set of accurately placed depth charges followed. Once *U505* surfaced, anti-personnel rather than armour-piercing ammunition was used to prevent the Germans from manning their guns and to encourage them to abandon their boat quickly, but without damaging it too heavily. This worked well. When the first boarding party arrived under the command of Lt Albert David, they found the only man left on the bridge to be dead. *U505,* still moving at about six knots and with the rudders jammed, had earlier created some drama by turning on *Chatelain* which fired a torpedo at the empty boat, thinking she was under attack.

Eventually, after some tricky manoeuvres in difficult seas, a boarding party from *Pillsbury* succeeded in getting on board. The central control room at the bottom of the ladder was already knee-deep in water, but this did not prevent the boarders from grabbing secret documents, books and the Enigma machine. Engineer's Mate Zenon Lukosius found water pouring in through a 20cm-diameter strainer, whose lid had been removed. Although he was already wading in water aboard a sinking submarine, he calmly set about searching for the cover, replaced it with considerable difficulty and thus prevented the boat from dropping further. In the meantime another boarding party from the *Guadalcanal* under Commander Earl Trosino arrived, making it quite a knees-up aboard *U505.*

At one stage, it looked as if the whole Hunter-Killer Group was coming on board, although that was not a terribly good idea because the boat was still sinking. As it settled lower and lower in the water, it quickly became apparent that stopping the boat's engines had not been a good idea. The hydroplanes were helping to keep it afloat, and stopping the forward motion made the boat settle even deeper. *Pillsbury* came alongside to lower some hoses with a view to pumping out the water. However, this did not go too well. Like others before her, she did not take the submarine's underwater hydroplanes into account. The destroyer came too close and a large hole was cut in her hull, flooding two of the bow compartments.

Above: The emergency steering wheel of *U505* with a repeater from the gyrocompass and an indicator to show the position of the rudder.

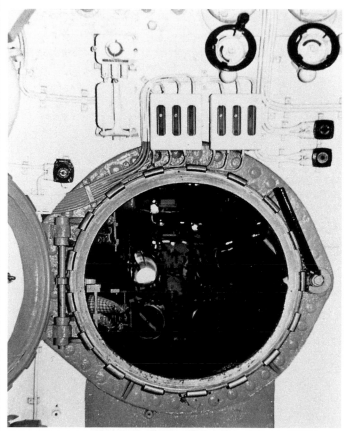

Above: The hatch leading into the forward torpedo compartment of *U505.*

U505 was eventually taken into tow by *Guadalcanal*, while the destroyers patrolled the surrounding waters in case other U-boats appeared. Gallery was for taking his prize to Dakar in Africa, the nearest friendly port, but he quickly received orders to go the other way and to attempt bringing it back to Bermuda. It was thought that there were too many German sympathisers in Africa to risk having *U505* seen there. *U505* had not used its radio and the American leadership was intent on preserving the secrecy of the occasion in order to gain maximum results from the captured material. It was thought that the boat's arrival in an African port would not be kept quiet for long and the fleet tug *Abnaki*, together with the tanker *Kennebec*, were dispatched to help with the 1,700-mile passage across the Atlantic.

U505 was eventually brought into Port Royal, Bermuda, on 19 June 1944. America had captured her first man-of-war since 1815. In the excitement the Americans claimed that *U505* was the first U-boat to have been boarded and captured. It is rather strange that this should have been written on a bronze plaque long after the war, when the authorities there must have known about the capture of *U570* more than two years earlier, but then official distortion of history had already become part of the daily process.

It would seem highly likely that Bletchley Park already knew much of what had been salvaged from *U505* and that the confidential material was only of limited value. However, the Americans were not going to be prevented from squeezing every ounce of glory from their effort and took *U505* for a prolonged tour of the United States after the war. Eventually, when the interest in the German submarine waned, the boat was left rotting in the US Navy Yard in Portsmouth, Virginia. Discovering that one of Chicago's sons had been involved in the capture, the city made an appeal to have the boat berthed there as a permanent war memorial. As a result, *U505* started her final voyage of 3,000 miles on 14 May 1954. Travelling up the St Lawrence river and through the Great Lakes, she eventually arrived on the shores of Lake Michigan. There the boat went into dry dock to have as much weight as possible removed. The remaining fuel oil and iron ballast was taken out to lighten her so that she could be pulled out of the water and across the road to lie by the side of the Science and Industry Museum, where she can still be inspected to this day.

The U-boat Command, having been battered by the D-Day invasion of Normandy, hardly noticed that *U505* had gone missing on its homeward-bound voyage. The boat continued to feature in the daily situation reports until the middle of July, when references vanished without comment about its loss. The survivors led a comparatively idyllic life until some time after the war, when they were repatriated to Germany.

Above: A circular pressure-resistant hatch through one of the bulkheads of *U505*. Above it is a loudspeaker of the boat's address system. This was coupled to the radio room and could be used for announcements or for relaying radio broadcasts.

Above: U505 after that fateful attack during the boat's fourth voyage. Much of the interior was wrecked as well, making the return voyage an exceptionally momentous undertaking. Although the boat was hardly capable of diving, the men succeeded in bringing it back to France.

Above: The seriously damaged *U505* photographed from the supply boat *U462* under Bruno Vowe.

Left: U505 in tow by USS *Guadalcanal* on its way back to Bermuda.
Imperial War Museum

Chapter 11
Other Secret Captures?

This chapter looks at other occasions when U-boats were nearly captured and during which it is just possible that secret materials may have been recovered by the Allied forces involved.

Secrets from U49

Bitter fighting around the northern town of Narvik, during the German invasion of Norway in 1940, resulted in the loss of 10 modern German destroyers. The aftermath of this battle was still in progress on 15 April when the British destroyers *Fearless* (Cdr K. L. Harkness) and *Brazen* (Lt-Cdr M. Culme-Seymour) came across *U49* nearby. Having sighted her, they used the cover of small islands to come relatively close, before charging in to deliver a fast, devastating attack with a number of depth charges. This was so accurate that the blast literally lifted the U-boat to the surface. There, a 4in shell passed through the conning tower while the commander was on top of it. Luckily for *U49*, the shell did not detonate until after it had come out on the other side, but despite this good fortune the signal-

Above: U53 was a Type VIIB, similar to *U49* from which papers were captured in Norway.

man behind the commander received serious shrapnel wounds in his stomach. Minutes later *U49* was abandoned. This much is generally agreed, but it has also been suggested that a number of secret papers were recovered, showing U-boat dispositions in Norway. However, contradictory evidence makes it difficult to be sure about this or to reconstruct the details of what actually happened.

One report has stated that the commander, Kptlt Curt von Gossler, gave the order to abandon ship shortly after he had recovered from the shock of the shell hit. The report continues that the majority of the crew donned life-jackets or escape apparatus, while a few remained behind to place the most obvious secret papers into a sack which was later thrown overboard. Unfortunately, it was not heavy enough and instead of sinking remained afloat long enough to be picked up by the Royal Navy.

However, one of the survivors, Obergefreiter Fritz Adam, told Commander Marcus E. Osen of the Royal Norwegian Navy in an interview long after the war, that he considered this version of events highly unlikely. He suggested that four men had remained on board to set scuttling charges.

There is also a further British report which states that men were shot at to prevent them from stuffing secret documents into a sack. Yet, it is unclear how an observer on a surface ship could determine this. If the men had a sack, they would hardly have negotiated the vertical ladder through the conning tower, with water pouring through at least two holes, holding books in their hands. Is it not more likely that they would have placed the books into the sack before climbing up?

It has also been said that men staggering about on the upper deck, steadying themselves by grabbing hold of the guns, made the destroyers think that this was an attempt at fighting back. In reply the Royal Navy supposedly did not economise with ammunition and also shot at men swimming in the water. However, only one man (Maschinenobergefreiter Wilhelm Lölsberg) was killed in the action, so this statement is also unlikely to be true.

Commander Osen also found two eyewitnesses in Sandsöy, his home town, who verified that the boat was brought most dramatically to the surface, amidst a hail of gunfire and reported that a sack containing U-boat clothing with rank badges was later washed ashore. A diary found in one of the pockets was supposedly sent to the police in Harstad. It is possible that this sack or kit bag gave rise to the secret papers story, or some documents might have been salvaged but it seems highly likely that whatever fell into Allied hands made only a minor, immediate contribution to the intelligence war.

Left: KptIt Curt von Gossler commissioning *U49* just a couple of weeks before the beginning of the war. Officers' greatcoats did not have piston rings, instead rank was displayed only by shoulder straps. Therefore he is wearing the full formal uniform with frock coat, which was not often seen aboard U-boats.

Below: The commissioning of *U49* in Kiel on 12 August 1939. In the foreground is a 20mm anti-aircraft gun. The Blücher Pier on the left has since been rebuilt, but the concrete foundations of this old structure are still visible.

The Bizarre End of *U501*

U501 was brought to the surface by well-placed depth charges so close to HMCS *Moosejaw* (Lt F. E. Grubb) that the German commander, Korvkpt Hugo Förster, stepped from his conning tower on to the deck of the Canadian corvette. This happened on 10 September 1941 shortly before midnight, when it was too dark to make out exactly what was happening. Fearing an armed boarding party, *Moosejaw* moved away from the stricken U-boat and raked it with gunfire, but it quickly became apparent that the men clambering out on to the deck were abandoning ship, rather than seeking a confrontation. Consequently *Moosejaw* went alongside once more with the intention of scrambling a boarding party. Another corvette, HMCS *Chambly* (Cdr J. S. Prentice), which had discovered the U-boat and dropped the first depth charges, was standing by in amazement, with men lining the deck wondering what was going to happen next. What actually did take place is difficult to reconstruct and both the German and Canadian versions are equally viable.

The Germans say that the interior had been prepared for scuttling and that the charges went off shortly after *Moosejaw* came alongside for the second time. This then caused the boat to go down rapidly. However, the Canadians claim that a boarding party, under the command of Lt Edward Simmons, got aboard *U501*, entered the central control room, but found it filling so rapidly with water that they withdrew again in somewhat of a hurry. Apparently one man, Stoker W.I. Brown, failed to get up the ladder in time and was sucked under with the U-boat. Whether anything of value was salvaged still remains a mystery, although the answer may lie somewhere among the material from Bletchley Park which is now in the Public Record Office in London. There is even some dispute about the number killed, with German accounts claiming 34 men were saved, while Allied records show the number to be 37.

The Loss of *U175*

It was good to be part of a successful boat and *U175* had a most auspicious first war cruise. Her commander, Kptlt Heinrich Bruns, became the central point of conversations in French cafés frequented by naval personnel. At the age of 30, he was older than the majority of his contemporaries. Service in the battleships *Scharnhorst* and *Schleswig-Holstein* had stood him in good stead, and a short spell in torpedo boats gave him the necessary small-ships' experience to help tackle the problems presented by a U-boat. After serving first as watch officer in *U75*, he commissioned *U175* in December 1941, just a few weeks before America's entry into the war. His first operational cruise took him across the Atlantic, into the Caribbean, where the

Above: Kptlt Heinrich Bruns, commander of *U175*, wearing U-boat leathers.

absence of effective U-boat defences offered the opportunities he had been seeking. Sadly, his crew did not share all of his enthusiasm. *U175* had left port in somewhat of a hurry without having been kitted out for the tropics and, with temperatures soaring as high as 50°C, this meant that rotting provisions quickly added a putrid stench to the men's daily chores.

Later, returning from their second war cruise, the men ran into Lorient in France to find the town devastated by a series of heavy air raids. Everybody knew that the Royal Air Force had been aiding the German war effort by missing naval installations and concentrating on bombing French houses, but this time it was different. The Saltzwedel Barracks for the 2nd U-Flotilla and the Hundius Compound for the 6th U-Flotilla were devastated. Even men sheltering in bunkers had been killed in addition to those caught in the open. Stepping back on land towards the end of February 1943, after having been in warm African waters, was a solemn affair made even worse by the chatter picked up in the cafés. Despite having had a slightly less successful voyage, Bruns was still the centre of conversation. He had fended off several attacks and his men had repaired serious damage at sea, allowing them a return to a hero's welcome. But this time the talk went deeper and at times hit harder at the nerves. Some said that Bruns had a 'sore throat', of the sort that could only be cured by hanging a Knight's Cross around it. He certainly was ambitious and comments that this would be more beneficial for the enemy than for Germany did not help to calm already shattered nerves. The men of *U175* had that deep-down feeling that things were bound to go wrong.

At 1100 hours on Saturday 17 April 1943, lookouts sighted convoy HX233. Bruns instantly shot ahead, prepared his boat for attack and dived. His officers, guessing what was on his mind, objected, saying it would be better to continue shadowing and to attack during the coming night, but Bruns pressed on. Taking a precautionary look while being overrun by the convoy he noticed an escort to the rear, but also the 11,752-ton United States tanker, *G. Harrison Smith*. It was not only the biggest ship in the convoy but also the largest he had met for some time. The chance of sinking it appeared to be good. The crew was at action stations. Torpedoes were ready. The target was only three-and-a-half kilometres away, the perfect range for a submerged attack. Ambition drove Bruns on to manoeuvre into a suitable firing position while the radio operator, working the sound gear, reported the high-pitched whine from destroyer engines getting increasingly loud. There was no need for him to repeat the observation. The noise soon became audible throughout the boat without the need for sensitive sound detection gear, but Bruns did not react to the threat. It was only when the Asdic pings were heard that he finally lost his nerve and turned away, but by that time it was too late.

The United States coastguard cutter *Spencer* had located *U175*. She moved in and straddled the target with 11 depth charges set between 15 and 30 metres. *U175* was still at a depth of 20 metres, right in the centre of the spread. When they detonated one after the other the men inside the U-boat were stunned. Lights went out, water squirted in, machinery failed and the boat plummeted into the depths. In the radio cabin the heavy equipment was ripped from its fittings, causing additional casualties as it hit the operators sitting below. There was no need to give orders. These calamities had been rehearsed under real war conditions. Even the poisonous fumes rising from the batteries were automatically neutralised by donning submarine escape apparatus. But this time things were considerably worse than before. The watertight doors could not be closed because the hull had been deformed. Even more serious, the depth gauges had smashed and the boat did not respond to the hydroplanes. Turning the huge manual control wheels did not arrest the steep downward plunge. Without waiting for permission, the engineering officer ordered the tanks to be blown.

Bruns did not countermand him. Instead he stood there, momentarily perplexed by the hammering still ringing in his ears. Seconds later, he reacted by climbing into the conning tower and up on to the bridge where he was met by a hail of gunfire. His remains were so badly mutilated that the men staggering up behind did not recognise the mass of flesh. Only a few, thrown on top of it, caught a glimpse of a finger with a distinctive ring, indicating it was the last remnant of their commander. Some reports state that the crew's panic had driven them into mass hysteria, which cannot be quite correct because a number of men remained below repairing damage, unaware that the order to abandon ship had been given. Perhaps it was their dedication which saved them. Despite *U175* not having made the slightest effort to shoot back, intense gunfire hit the men now swimming in the water. In the uncontrolled barrage one American seaman was killed by his own side and at least one ship in the convoy suffered considerable damage. Their own side described the gunners as a rabble and noted that some men even loitered in front of guns in order to get a good view of the action.

Below: U175, a Type IXC, under attack with Convoy HX233 in the distance.

Above: Survivors from *U175* aboard the United States coastguard cutter *Spencer*.

Left: Moments before, the ramming course towards *U175* was called off in favour of an attempt to board the sinking U-boat. The launchers and projectiles of the ahead-throwing anti-submarine mortar can be seen in the foreground.

Left: U175's page in the Guests' Book of the 5th U-boat Flotilla. This flotilla supplied new operational boats with provisions — so the majority of boats passed through it. In translation, the page reads: 'Despite ice, appendicitis, trials, despite periscope damage and engagements at last we are ready to show that after finishing-off work and being kitted out we have a determined mind to win. Many Thanks!'. It is signed by *U175*'s four officers.

There has been some debate about the ferociousness of this attack. One report justified the bloodbath with the comment that the men from the sinking U-boat failed to hoist a white flag. Possibly German retaliation was also over-exaggerated to cover up the damage, killing and injuries caused to the gunners' own side. The guns continued shooting for some time after the order to cease fire had been given and the last few men from *U175* jumped into sporadic rather than hailing gunfire. In the end the death toll was not as terrific as the noisy display might have suggested and only 13 men lost their lives.

A boarding party of six men managed to row over to the U-boat and get on board. Their motor cutter could not be used because that had been holed by the friendly fire. It appeared as if a number of merchant ships used their guns as well, without a great deal of regard as to where their shells were landing. Boarding was not easy and the men had hardly achieved the feat when a signal from *Spencer* told them to stay off, but by this time the first men were on the top of the conning tower, horrified by the butcher's shop appearance. When the hatch was opened, the boat seemed suddenly to sink deeper, so a hand grenade was thrown in to kill anyone left on board and then the boarding party withdrew. It seems highly unlikely that anyone climbed down inside and presumably therefore nothing of value was retrieved.

The Prolonged Hunt for *U744*

Oberleutnant-zur-See Heinz Blischke died a slow and horrific death, but his ability, cunning and determination saved the majority of his crew. His final action started while stalking convoy HX280, plodding eastwards at nine knots. Unfortunately for *U744*, the Canadian destroyer *Gatineau* had stopped a little distance away from the merchant ships in order to overhaul its freshwater still. (This produced pure water to drive the steam turbines, therefore the repairs were of a most critical nature.) Although effectively a sitting duck, *Gatineau* maintained Asdic sweeps, which quickly produced a positive echo. Unable to do much about it herself, the news was flashed over to the escort commander in the destroyer *St Catherines*, who raced over to drop 10 depth charges. At the same time, the convoy changed course to head further north and avoid the intruder. *Gatineau's* faint echo marked the beginning of one of the longest U-boat hunts and what happened next is best described by the following table. Ironically, though, the damage aboard *Gatineau* could not be repaired; consequently she was sent back to Northern Ireland without seeing the end of the action which she started.

5 March 1944

TIME	ESCORT	WEAPON USED AND REMARKS
0400		*U744* dived.
1000	*Gatineau*	Detected *U744* with Asdic.
1028	*St Catherines*	10 depth charges dropped. No response.
1137	*Chilliwack*	Hedgehog fired. (An ahead-throwing mortar whose shells detonated only on impact.) No hits.
1236	*Gatineau*	22 depth charges dropped during a creeping attack directed by *St Catherines*.
1244	*Chilliwack*	22 depth charges dropped.
1305	*Gatineau*	Hedgehog fired, no detonations.
1316	*Gatineau*	Mark X depth charge fired, but failed to detonate.
1350	*Chilliwack*	26 depth charges dropped during a creeping attack with *St Catherines* directing *Chilliwack* to the correct spot.
1357	*Icarus*	Hedgehog fired, no detonations.
1458	*Kenilworth Castle*	Three Squid fired (also an ahead-throwing mortar whose bombs detonated only on impact). No hits.
1538	*Kenilworth Castle*	Three Squid fired, but no detonations.
1642	*Fennel*	21 depth charges dropped while directed by *St Catherines*.
1656	*St Catherines*	22 depth charges dropped.
1920	*Kenilworth Castle*	Three Squid fired, no detonations.
2018	*Fennel*	22 depth charges dropped
2029	*St Catherines*	19 depth charges dropped.

6 March 1944

TIME	ESCORT	WEAPON USED AND REMARKS
0023	*St Catherines*	10 depth charges dropped.
0041	*St Catherines*	10 depth charges dropped.
0109	*Fennel*	Hedgehog fired, no detonations.
0751	*Fennel*	Hedgehog fired, no detonations.
0829	*Icarus*	Hedgehog fired, no detonations.
1004	*Chaudière*	26 depth charges dropped while directed by *St Catherines*.
1013	*St Catherines*	22 depth charges dropped while directed by *Icarus*.
1050	*Chaudière*	26 depth charges dropped.
1100	*Icarus*	24 depth charges dropped.
1532	All ships	*U744* surfaces and is met with gunfire. 10 rounds from 105mm, 97 rounds from 40mm, 480 rounds from 20mm and 450 from other calibres fired. *U744* was abandoned and later sunk by torpedo from *Icarus*.

The escorts were:

Destroyers:	HMCS *Gatineau* (Lt-Cdr H. V. W. Groos)
	HMCS *Chaudière* (Lt-Cdr C. P. Nixon)
	HMCS *Icarus* (Lt-Cdr R. Dyer)
Frigates:	HMCS *St Catherines* (Lt-Cdr H. C. R. Davis) with the escort groups' commander (P. W. Burnett RN) on board.
	HMCS *Fennel* (Lt-Cdr W. P. Moffat)
	HMCS *Chilliwack* (Lt-Cdr G. R. Coughlin)
Corvette:	HMS *Kenilworth Castle* (Lt J. J. Allon)

The men in *U744* heard the 'pings' of *Gatineau's* Asdic, as well as the high-pitched whine of the approaching destroyer. The splashes of depth charges hitting the water could also be heard throughout the boat without the need of the sensitive sound detector. Blischke reacted to the first attack by turning into *St Catherines'* wake, with the hope of hiding in the disturbance she herself was creating. Of course, he could hardly keep up such a burst of speed and it was not too long before the destroyer was far enough away to get another Asdic bearing on the submerged submarine.

U744's first watch officer Hellmuth Jonas, who later served in the Federal German Navy as a Fregattenkapitän, has recorded his impressions of this fateful event and Franz Selinger, a distinguished Austrian historian living in Germany, has also written a detailed description of the sinking. Jonas said that despite the tension and the immense hammering, there was no panic in the boat. There was no food either because extreme silence had been ordered. The men could not risk giving away their position by clanking cooking utensils. Unfortunately for them, the ventilation system also broke down during one of the early attacks, meaning that they had to wear breathing masks, an uncomfortable addition to the already unbearable situation. Each time another escort could be heard moving in to drop depth charges Blischke coolly ordered a change of course at the fastest possible speed to avoid the main blast of the impact. That he succeeded in keeping this up for the best part of 30 hours is a terrific achievement, showing that both he and his men had learned their trade very well indeed. With the air becoming staler and staler, however, every action required a superhuman effort. Many men wished that the next blast would hit, to put them out of the misery of the most horrific of experiences. Yet, despite becoming painfully lethargic, they maintained their watchfulness and sharp reactions.

At three o'clock in the afternoon of the second day, Blischke discussed possible options with the men in the control room. The engineering officer, Günter Dreissig, who was killed shortly afterwards, assured Blischke that there was enough power in the batteries for another two to three hours, perhaps even longer. It depended on how often he had to use top speed. There was little hope of the pursuers giving up. They were clearly set on hunting the boat to destruction and there appeared to be no hope of escaping during the coming darkness. In fact, the coming night was seen as a definite disadvantage. There would be little chance of anyone being rescued, especially as the surface of the ocean appeared to be becoming increasingly turbulent and it was thought that the surface ships would not search for survivors during such a choppy night. The air in the boat was foul beyond imagination, with the carbon dioxide indicator suggesting human life was no longer possible. Staying down would result in certain death. No one knew what might happen if they surfaced, but there was a faint glimmer of hope that at least the men's lives might be spared.

Chilliwack was in the process of embarking upon another run-in to drop depth charges when *U744* broke surface. The tanks having been filled with compressed air, the U-boat appeared to have been glued high on the choppy water. No one inside the boat had any idea what was happening on the outside and the conning tower hatch, the only way out, took some time to open. While Blischke was struggling with the locking mechanism, it became apparent that *U744* had become the centre of an intense artillery action. Eventually, having reached the top of the conning tower, Blischke could see he no longer had any guns left for possible retaliatory action. The only sensible action was to abandon ship. The order had hardly left his mouth when he fell mortally wounded, to bleed to death. Ammunition already being prepared for carrying up to the top of the conning tower was dropped while everybody concentrated on getting out. At the same time, scuttling charges were set. The men had 10 minutes to jump overboard, but the majority were so exhausted by the long lack of air that it was a slow, painful process to climb up and face that hail of bullets. During the next minutes, while everybody was more than preoccupied trying to remain alive, things happened rather quickly. The scuttling charges appeared also to suffer from a shortage of fresh air. Ten minutes passed without any sign of a detonation. Most of the men were so exhausted that they could hardly stand up when they were rescued. Those that died probably suffered from total exhaustion, rather than being hit by the intense gunfire directed at them.

What happened next is difficult to ascertain. *Chilliwack* definitely succeeded in launching a whaler despite the atrocious conditions and it is a great credit that some of her men managed to get on board the U-boat. The first man on board, Signalman J. R. Starr, seemed more interested in hoisting a flag rather than climbing below to salvage secret documents. Lt Atherton, Lt Hearn and Petty Officer Longbottom did reach the central control room, but water was rising fast. One account states that they retreated immediately afterwards and another states that they recovered a number of important secret items, including the Enigma machine. Whatever may be the truth, the whaler capsized shortly afterwards, throwing men and contents into the water, meaning that the secrets were forgotten in favour of an all-out rescue attempt to save as many as possible. Reports that a tow rope was fastened to the U-boat seem highly improbable and have been disputed by a number of serious researchers, including Korvkpt Jonas.

This prolonged hunt leading to the sinking of *U744* is one of those examples where both sides fought the most fraught and determined battle under difficult conditions. Everybody handled their part with incredible bravery. The men in the U-boat, in the escorts and especially the boarding party offered their country more than the usual call of duty, making this one of the great achievements of the war. There is just one little mysterious twist in the tail of this magnificent accomplishment. It was in everybody's interest that the captured material should have been officially described as lost at sea. It got the Germans off the hook of having had their boat boarded and for the Allies it added extra security had anything been captured. One wonders whether everything really did go down when that whaler capsized.

Below: ObltzS Heinz Blischke of *U744*, shooting the sun.

Left: ObltzS Heinz Blischke of *U744* wearing a white hat. The caps worn by the other men, called the 'Schiffchen' or 'Small Ship' type, were favoured because they folded flat.

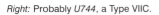

Right: Probably *U744*, a Type VIIC.

Chapter 12
The Sinking and Raising of *U250*

The most powerful of all opposition, the unpredictable weather, played a major role in the sinking and raising of *U250*. Dead calm, crystal clear water with a brilliant sun shining down some 30–40 metres to the yellowish sea bed helped the Russians in sinking her and, later, fog allowed them to raise the wreck from under the noses of Finnish coastal batteries. Bringing *U250* into the naval base at Kronshtadt, was an incredible achievement unequalled during the war. All other submarines which fell into enemy hands did so on the surface. No one else raised an enemy wreck.

U250's commander for her short career was Werner-Karl Schmidt, who must not be confused with Werner von Schmidt nor with Werner Schmidt. He had been seconded to the Luftwaffe and had even piloted bombers over Russia and Britain. When he started his submarine training, German forces at Stalingrad had just surrendered, marking a major turning point of the war. Schmidt then held a number of land-based positions before commissioning *U250* two weeks before Christmas of 1943. Trials and working-up periods had already been reduced to way below the minimum, so that six months later the boat was on her way to the 5th U-boat Flotilla in Kiel for final kitting out. Plans for sailing west were suddenly cancelled. The Obersteuermann (Navigator) was recalled from his Atlantic briefing, told to collect charts of the Gulf of Finland and to make sure he had maps of all the major ports there.

So far the eastern Baltic had been a safe haven for U-boat training, but the summer of 1944 saw some drastic changes, with bitter battles being fought along a minefield which was locking the Russians into the so-called 'Bathtub' off Finland. Earlier in the war German forces had penetrated as far as Leningrad, but never succeeded in capturing the city. Living and fighting with the barest of materials under the most unimaginably primitive circumstances, the ragged force of local resistance kept the might of the German Army at bay. Now the Red Army was forcing the Germans back at Leningrad and all along the front and, at the same time, remnants of the Russian navy emerged from its hiding places to create havoc along the Baltic shores. When the comparatively small naval units in the eastern Baltic could no longer restrain their Russian counterparts, Konteradmiral Theodor Burchardi, Commanding Officer of the Eastern Baltic, had no choice other than to request reinforcements. Consequently *U250* became one of several U-boats to sail into the hated shallow waters of the Gulf of Finland. These are only about 100km across, which meant there

was not much room for manoeuvre and the water was not deep enough to get away from serious depth charge detonations. In fact, the dreaded area contained all the features for a submariner's worst nightmare.

One consoling point may well have been a lack of opposition determination in driving home its attacks and the first attack against *U250* was in a similar vein. Having been caught by the tiny, 56-ton, patrol boat *MO105* under Lt Georgi Schwaljuk, *U250* experienced a half-hearted depth charge attack. The disturbance from this enabled Schmidt to withdraw to a safe distance. Very much to his surprise, the hunter did not pursue him. Instead, the tiny cockle-shell patrol boat called off the hunt for lunch. Not only that, but its engines were shut down as well so that the men could enjoy a refreshing swim. It was a hot day at the end of July 1944, when those inviting waters were at their best. *MO105* was so small that it was scarcely even worth a torpedo and shooting one would certainly draw attention to the U-boat in the shallow coastal waters. But Schmidt thought that, since he was close to a well-known minefield, the opposition would probably assume that little *Moschka*, as the patrol boats were affectionately known, had hit one of these. Unfortunately for him, he was mistaken. The Russians had already occupied a number of small islands off the Finnish coast and an observation post on one of these reported the sinking. Within minutes, another similar patrol boat, *MO103* under Alexander Petrovic Kolenko, led the way to challenge the U-boat.

Nikolai Bondar, a sailor aboard a minesweeper, spotted the shadow of the grey hulk in the depths and thus quickly confirmed that the earlier detonation had not been caused by a mine. His ship was not equipped with anti-submarine weapons and therefore could not take advantage of the situation. Instead the men waited anxiously for *MO103* to drop depth charges. Being unable to avoid the onslaught, the men in *U250* could only hope that this hunter lost interest as quickly as the first. But this time they were out of luck. Kolenko knew there was a submarine below him and he was not the type to give up easily. The situation inside *U250* quickly became desperate. The first detonation damaged some of the machinery and then a direct hit on the engine room tore a massive hole in the hull, allowing the interior to fill with water so quickly that there was nothing anyone could do to prevent it. Schmidt and five other men in the central control room, standing up to their necks in water, were saved by a small pocket of air at the top of the boat. Although stunned, they did have the presence of

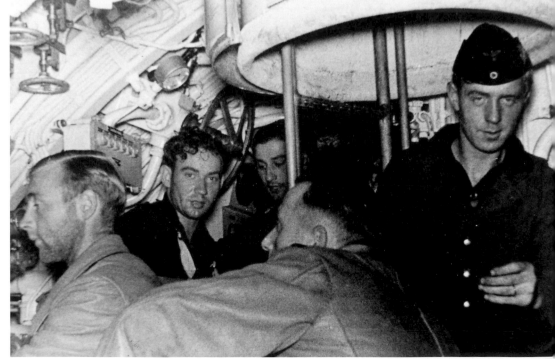

Above: The commissioning of *U250* by Werner-Karl Schmidt. The boat has been fitted with the new gun platforms but the armament has not yet been installed. The open galley hatch is visible at the base of the Wintergarten.

Right: The central control room of an unidentified boat with vertical ladder leading up into the conning tower compartment and on to the open bridge above it. The tube visible above the head of the man on the right saved the lives of a few survivors from *U250* by trapping enough air for them to breathe until they could make their way out, up the ladder.

mind to blow the diving tanks in the hope of bringing the boat to the surface. This was done by opening the taps of compressed air bottles without having to run any machinery and operators were trained to perform such tasks in total darkness. The flooded control room added considerable difficulties, but the taps turned, although no one could see the depth gauges any more and therefore the men had no idea whether this was having any effect or not. They did not have a great deal of choice. They could either drown where they were or make their way up through the conning tower to the main hatch. Surprisingly, all six had managed this tricky manoeuvre when another deafening roar stunned them into temporary unconsciousness. Patrol boat MO103 was not letting go and assumed the wreck on the seabed might still escape. Therefore another depth charge was sent down for good measure. This tore the hatch from its fittings, allowing a massive air bubble to burst to the surface, bringing with it all six men from the conning tower. Kolenko had just picked them up when the Finnish coastal batteries took an interest in the commotion and opened fire to drive the Russians away.

Making his getaway, Kolenko realised he had achieved something of a coup. Never before, and never again afterwards, did survivors from a U-boat fall into Russian hands. None of his prisoners offered any information of value, but Kolenko thought that the men might yield some vital intelligence if they were treated properly. Cdr Dmitri Woinalvic, Head of the Interrogation Department, shared this view and took on the questioning himself. Instead of brute force, he decided that cunning, patience and determination would yield the best results. He seems to have been right. He also guessed that the wreck might yield more secrets and suggested that divers should be sent down to examine the interior.

This was not as easy as it may sound. Not only was U250 lying within range of Finnish coastal batteries (the Germans and Finns were allies), but the Germans had also been informed of the sinking and had taken precautions to prevent inquisitive Russians from reaching the U-boat. U250 was located by the Kriegsmarine and plastered with depth charges before mines were laid around it. In a way this effort made the Russians even more determined, thinking there must be something of value to be had from the wreck. Creeping out there at night, divers found U250 to be lying virtually upright on the seabed with little apparent damage to the torpedo tubes or the important control compartments in the middle of the boat. Despite enormous problems, the divers entered the central control room and rummaged about in the commander's 'cabin' to bring back charts, books, private papers and photographs.

Following this, divers dug two tunnels under the boat, passed hawsers through them, brought in lifting gear and brought U250 back to the surface right under the noses of enemy artillery. Using darkness and fog as a cover, the U-boat was slowly lifted off the bottom and then, when visibility improved, ships sailed between the sinking site and the coastal batteries to lay an artificial fog screen. Moving at a speed of one or two knots, it took several days before the prize was finally brought into the naval base on the fortified island at Kronshtadt.

Werner Schmidt stood with considerable trepidation by the edge of the dry dock, watching the last of the water drip from the battered remains of his old command. The Russians were anxious to get inside, but had discovered a series of special destruction charges laid along the length of the hull and therefore expected there to be more booby traps inside. No one fancied taking the risk of blowing themselves and their most valuable prize sky-high and preferred Schmidt to lead the way. These self-destruct mechanisms were nothing more than the damaged heads of the underwater sound detectors, but Schmidt did not enlighten his captors. Although doing everything that was asked of him, he and his men remained so quiet about naval secrets that higher authorities insisted that painful pressure be brought to bear on the prisoners to make them reveal more information. Yet, despite these demands, neither Schmidt nor the other five survivors were deliberately mistreated.

Entering the boat was no easy matter. The interior was dark, wet and reeking of fuel oil. So much so, that Schmidt later felt sick and asked to leave again. The black interior still contained 46 corpses who had died under excruciatingly painful circumstances and had now been bloated by water. Not only did they look hideous, but a good number of eels wriggled through them, adding an even more horrific atmosphere to an already frightening scene. The Enigma machine was lying on the table in the radio room and to Schmidt's surprise many of the secret books, including the all-important codes, were still in reasonable condition. The ink had not dissolved nor had the paper disintegrated. Picking them up and flicking through the books, he could still read much of the text. The only consolation was that the codes were now several weeks old and would soon be out of date.

To his surprise, the Russians showed only a superficial interest in the sophisticated coding system, being far more enthusiastic about the acoustic torpedo of Type Zaunkönig or T5, of which there were several on board. These had been in service since the summer of the previous year and were thought to have been highly successful. Even modern Russian accounts maintain this image, although in reality only about 10% of them functioned the way they should have done. Britain had been aware of this built-in fault since early in the year, but still wanted to examine such torpedoes at first hand. Despite an impenetrable cloud of secrecy hanging over many Russian activities, the Admiralty in London became aware of the raising and that some T5 torpedoes had fallen into Russian hands. The British Prime Minister, Winston Churchill, himself sent a lengthy telegram to Josef Stalin, the Russian leader, asking permission for British naval officers to examine them.

By that time the Red Army's westward move was gaining momentum and there was no longer anything which could stop it. It was just a matter of time until Hitler was crushed. Stalin knew that he could win on his own, without support from the western allies. He could afford to be uncooperative and dragged matters out until permission was finally given. Then, when an invitation was forthcoming, it took three months for the necessary visas to be issued. This obstinacy was not all. When things looked as if they were going ahead, the Russians prohibited direct access to Kronshtadt, saying the short route was too dangerous. Instead, they insisted that the British visitors travelled via Persia. When they finally arrived at

the naval base, they were only allowed to look at the torpedoes from a distance. The Cold War had already effectively begun. The Russians were not going to help their western allies and the Royal Navy officers returned empty handed.

It is now difficult to determine what if any value the Soviets actually squeezed out of the Enigma machine and the radio secrets, but by late 1944 Britain was hardly dependent on a third party to understand German radio signals. By this stage Bletchley Park was often reading enemy signals faster than the intended recipients. In fact there were many occasions when signals arrived at British command posts a considerable time before German commanders saw the same information.

Below: U250 in dry dock after having been raised by the Russians. The boat appears to be in reasonable condition, with hardly any significant damage.

Above: U250 looks in remarkably good condition, especially when one considers what it had been through to get into this dry dock.

Left: This close-up of the damage to the engine room section of *U250* explains why the boat went down so exceptionally quickly.

Chapter 13
Salvaging Secrets

A recently declassified document generated considerable excitement by disclosing that secrets had been salvaged from *U415*. This startling news had not been made public before and, as the boat was sunk a short while after the D-Day invasion of Normandy, it could well have yielded some vital advantages for Bletchley Park. However, the high spirits were short-lived. Another glance into the records revealed that the secrets were salvaged by the Germans rather than the Allies and there was no way that any of the confidential material found its way to Britain or the United States. Yet, despite the anticlimax, the comment sparked off a thorough search through dust-covered documents to check whether the Allies could have salvaged secrets from other U-boats.

U415 under ObltzS Herbert Werner (author of the book *Iron Coffins*) was sunk a short distance in front of the massive U-boat bunker in Brest. *U415* had survived a bid to attack the invasion supply routes but only just managed to crawl back to base with help from *U256* (ObltzS Wilhelm Brauel). Repairs then kept *U415* in dock until mid-August 1944 when sea trials were fixed for the early hours of the 16th. Everything went well, except that Werner overslept during that crucial morning and therefore failed to appear at the appointed time. Somewhat annoyed, the flotilla engineer ordered the first watch officer, Karl-Heinz Meinert, to move the boat out into the dock basin where they were going to wait for the commander. As has already been mentioned, watch officers were not necessarily acquainted with the standard procedures and Meinert did not know that diesel engines should not be started within the harbour area. By doing so, he activated an acoustic mine dropped by an aircraft a few days earlier. Werner was on his way down from his accommodation when he saw the boat engulfed by a massive fountain of water, while two men (Wolfgang Brandt and Heinz Wegat) were hurled high into the air. Surprisingly the rest of the crew survived, although eight were seriously injured.

A French salvage firm was brought in to raise the wreck while *U415*'s engineering officer, Christian Brede, supervised the recovery of secret materials. He and a number of Germans were the first to enter the still dripping interior for the sole purpose of laying their hands on the Enigma machine and other confidential documents. Such books had their serial number embossed on the cover or on the first page, so everything could be checked off on the boat's inventory and handed back to the naval stores before foreign workers were allowed inside. The thoroughness with which this was carried out illustrates how much emphasis the Germans put on their secrets, making it exceedingly difficult for non-crew members to gain access to classified material.

Although the Enigma machine from *U415* remained in German hands, a few months later one was found floating on the surface of the Atlantic. This happened during April 1945, just weeks before the end of the war, when an Irish fisherman spotted a container bobbing among the waves near the Fastnet Rock off the coast of County Cork. On opening it, he discovered a top secret codewriter together with a number of confidential books. By that time it was well known that *U260* (ObltzS Klaus Becker) had been sunk by a mine and that the crew had been interned in Ireland. So, it was easy to guess where the material had come from. Newspapers had reported how the Germans struggled for a couple of days to keep their heavily damaged boat afloat before abandoning it in Irish territorial waters and paddling ashore. It would appear that the men in *U260* either did not have, or could not use, the usual lead-lined sacks for jettisoning sensitive material and packed this inside an ammunition container. It is quite likely that this was done in the dark and that the crew failed to notice that the package did not sink. Even if these secrets had ended up at Bletchley Park, they would have been of little use because by that time Britain was decoding Kriegsmarine signals quicker than the Germans.

Other records of Enigma machines falling into Allied hands have not been found. Of course, had this happened, the matter would hardly have been disclosed at the time or for many years after. What is more, all the participants in such a drama could have been killed before the end of the war, thus shutting the lid of confidentiality even tighter. In view of this high level of secrecy, some historians have thought it worth while to hunt through the records for any clues of possible recoveries, although the fact that nothing has ever leaked out would suggest that this is an exceedingly remote possibility. This search for evidence of secrets having been salvaged has been most interesting. Old records have revealed that all manner of confidential and personal matter floated to the surface when boats were sunk. A close depth charge detonation would have had a similar effect to a balloon bursting. The hull might break up with such a large hole being blown that the mass of escaping air could carry even quite heavy objects to the surface. Of course, it was unlikely for an Enigma machine to be lifted, but papers and masses of other objects were recovered throughout the course of the war. With this in mind, a number of

Above: U260, the boat which sank in Irish territorial waters, with the later type of armoured conning tower and schnorkel bracket below the feet of the man sitting on the top. Note the portable radio behind him and the head lens of the partly raised attack periscope.

destroyers dropped depth charges on U-boats sunk in shallow waters to open their hulls. So, could this have yielded anything of value?

U247 (ObltzS Gerhard Matschulat) produced most startling results. Oil floating to the surface was not considered good enough to confirm a kill, so the frigate *St John* (Lt-Cdr W. R. Stacey) carefully searched the area near Land's End where *U247* had been located. After finding the apparently stationary wreck, five depth charges were dropped to make certain that the U-boat could not escape. One wonders what the men on *St John's* deck must have thought when various items of clothing including a leather coat, photographs, papers and a variety of other pieces floated to the surface. One of these, looking like an official document, was nothing more than a 'fun' certificate to mark the boat's 10 millionth propeller revolution. Yet, making the effort to pick up the debris was worth while because a wiring diagram of the radio also appeared and this made it possible to identify the U-boat.

Not all attacks on stationary wrecks went off without incident. HMCS *Chaudière* (Lt-Cdr C. P. Nixon), for example, fired two Hedgehogs after having obtained excellent contacts on the wreck of *U621* (ObltzS Hermann Stuckmann). A number of gloves and a letter floated to the surface, encouraging Nixon to have another go at opening up the boat, with the hope of recovering some secrets.

Once again at least one of the projectiles detonated, but this time it also triggered off an explosion in the wreck, showering the surface with a massive, unexpected and most impressive fountain of water, but unfortunately without releasing any more noteworthy wreckage.

One aspect of the war at sea was that men rarely saw the people on the other side. Kills were made over long distances, almost as if by remote control. Yet, despite this, there were a number of highly macabre happenings. Flight Lieutenant G. W. Parker, flying Liberator 'N' from No 86 Squadron, RAF, straddled the surfaced *U317* (ObltzS Peter Rahlff) so accurately with depth charges that he could watch the boat turn over and disappear. Almost instantly a massive pool of oil appeared and then, one after another, men started floating around in the muck. None of them moved and when Parker flew over for a close inspection it looked as if they had all been killed by the blast.

Men in the United States escorts *Inch* (Lt-Cdr W. C. Frey) and *Frost* (Lt-Cdr J. H. McWhorter) found themselves in a similar situation after having sunk *U154* (ObltzS Gerth Gemeiner), only this time they were not cruising through dead bodies, but bits and pieces such as arms, legs and torsos. Some films and books dealing with blood and guts give the impression of sailors being delighted at having destroyed the opposition, but by talking to men who actually experienced such morbid situations it becomes clear that many were horrified by such sickening encounters.

Among the list of bizarre sinkings, where secret documents could have been recovered, one needs to consider the singularly peculiar case of *U413* (ObltzS Dietrich Sachse) which was discovered during a routine search by the destroyer HMS *Vidette* (Lt-Cdr G. S. Woolley). The incident could have been observed from the top of Beachy Head on the English south coast near Eastbourne and came about as a result of *U413* giving away its position by torpedoing a freighter. The subsequent attack by *Vidette*, HMS *Forester* (Cdr G. W. Gregory) and HMS *Wensleydale* (Lt-Cdr W. P. Goodfellow) brought quick results. First, an oil slick indicated that the boat had almost certainly been hit; there was too much of it to have been jettisoned on purpose. Then, suddenly and quite unexpectedly, one solitary man appeared, but his loss of consciousness soon after rescue meant he could not provide any useful information. Rather than wait for more men to come up, another devastating attack was launched.

The man was ObltzS (Ing) Karl Hütterer, the engineering officer, and it is quite likely that if he were to write his story as a piece of fiction, readers would declare it to be too far-fetched, saying it could never have happened. In fact, the story he told sounds implausible and impossible, yet he was the living proof that it did actually happen. The boat was proceeding close to periscope depth with Oblt Sachse sitting on the saddle by the attack periscope inside the conning tower control room. Sachse followed his own standing instructions and had the hatch closed between him and the central control room below his feet. From down below it sounded as if the first depth charge removed the conning tower together with the commander and a petty officer who was there for relaying orders and possibly working the torpedo calculator.

Hütterer found it impossible to open the hatch above him. At the same time, large volumes of water were pouring down, filling up the central control room. The boat settled on the seabed and the rising water drove the men forward to the bow torpedo room. There they waited until there was sufficient water in the boat to equalise the outside pressure. Luckily they were not terribly deep and two of the torpedo tubes were still empty from the earlier attack, leaving everybody with a good chance of escaping from their iron coffin. Opening both ends of the tubes, Hütterer led the way by crawling through, feeling in the darkness for any possible obstructions. There was nothing to bar the way, so he expected the rest of the crew to follow him to the surface. Unfortunately, something in the dark, cold and wet broke the delicate human chain, for no one else appeared. In the end, only a variety of

books, papers and other gear were recovered by the surface ships.

After Hütterer reached the surface hydrophone operators aboard the British ships apparently heard noises of tanks being blown, giving them the impression that the U-boat's remaining crewmen were starting the machinery to escape and the ships launched into the final devastating attack, sealing the fate of any survivors down below.

A few weeks earlier, a similar hunt had taken place to the south of Brighton, only a short distance away. Escort Group 11, comprising the British corvette *Statice* (Lt R. Wolfendon) and Canadian destroyers *Ottawa* (Capt J. Prentice) and *Kootenay* (Lt-Cdr W. H. Wilson), was busy hunting in the shallow Channel waters but only finding old wrecks, when *Statice* made contact with a suspected submarine. It was moving in the same direction as the tide and with the same speed, but unlike earlier contacts, it was at least moving. The firing of the Hedgehog produced a detonation, which would suggest that a projectile had hit something. What was more, the target now changed direction, indicating quite clearly that this was something intelligent with its own will. A further attack produced a good number of German novels, some papers and what looked like a textbook example of a dissected human lung. All this, together with a good saturation of oil, was still considered to have been insufficient evidence of a kill and further searches led to more attacks. In the end, *Ottawa* even towed a cable with grappling hook to locate the wreck and to plaster it with more depth charges. Much of this effort seems to have been unnecessary. Capt Prentice should have known that it is highly unlikely for any submarine to survive two Hedgehog hits, and those projectiles were designed to detonate only on contact. Therefore the explosions had to be hits and could not have been near-misses. The victim this time was *U678* under ObltzS Guido Hyronimus.

Another boat worth considering for a possible recovery of an Enigma machine was *U1209* (ObltzS Ewald Hülsenbeck), which was stranded on the Wolf Rock in the Isles of Scilly. The boat was submerged when this happened so obviously it was impossible for anyone to have got inside at that point. This happened on 18 December 1944, at a time when it was hardly necessary to risk the lives of Royal Navy divers for the exceedingly difficult undertaking of diving in treacherous currents. Bletchley Park was already reading German signals without any significant problems.

These examples given here are by no means the only ones. The records are littered with a good many similar cases which makes one wonder whether significant secrets did reach the Allies from sinking wrecks. One also wonders what has happened to those insignificant items which were captured. Perhaps they are still somewhere, serving as forgotten heirlooms of Europe's most turbulent period.

Chapter 14
U1024 — The Last Capture

The capture of *U1024* was just as remarkable as the *U110* incident, but the hoard was instantly devalued four weeks later when the war ended.

In July 1943 the Allied air forces launched a devastating attack on the city of Hamburg, aiming their bombs at residential districts where they killed as many women, children and old people in a couple of weeks as Britain lost during the entire war. Over 100,000 more were badly injured and unimaginable numbers were made homeless, losing all their possessions. Only a few weeks before all this, *U1024*'s keel had been laid at Blohm und Voss in Hamburg and a short while later most of her crew started their submarine training. Yet, despite the damage in the town, *U1024* was completed in record time, to be launched a good 30 days quicker than boats which had been built before this dreadful attack.

U1024's commander, Kapitänleutnant Hans-Joachim Gutteck, was an officer of the Reserve, who had served with land-based heavy artillery units until 1943 when he was drafted into *Sperrbrecher*. He started his submarine training some four months after *U1024*'s keel had been laid. Although he was not in Hamburg at the time of the terror attack, the cloud of destruction hanging over the city blacked out the sun along the Baltic coast, some 100km away, where he was taking his first steps to become a submariner. He can hardly be classed as an experienced commander, yet despite this, he displayed a great deal of courage, determination and skill, extracting his boat from precarious predicaments which would have taxed even long-serving aces.

U1024 left Kiel for Norway on 30 December 1944. Some vital finishing-off work was then carried out in Horten and schnorkelling was practised in the Norwegian fjords, making it early March 1945 before the boat left for its first and only operational mission in the Irish Sea. The schnorkel was a hinged breathing pipe for running the diesel engines below the surface of the water. Although several authors have recently heralded this as a fantastic invention for regaining a foothold in the convoy war, in reality the device provided nothing more than the difference between a quick death and the meagrest of painful survivals. Schnorkelling reduced the top speed to a maximum of about five knots and progress was often considerably slower, meaning there was no way it could be used to chase convoys. At best, *U1024* could cover only about 150km per day, so it took a while before she reached her operations area in the Irish Sea. The breathing system frequently leaked, allowing poisonous carbon monoxide into the boat. This was so bad at times that some boats were forced to surface in order to prevent everybody being gassed into unconsciousness. The only advantage *U1024* found in the Irish Sea was a mirror smooth surface, allowing the batteries to be charged without waves washing over the top of the head valve and thereby shutting off the air supply. This created such an uncomfortable difference in air pressure that some men had their ear drums permanently damaged.

Attacking two freighters between Anglesey and the Isle of Man was very much to Gutteck's disadvantage because it definitely confirmed the presence of a U-boat. Being in relatively shallow waters with a good proportion of debris on the seabed, however, meant that his hunters were frequently attracted to older wrecks and started depth charging these instead of *U1024*. Whatever

Above: KptIt Hans-Joachim Gutteck, commander of *U1024*, was killed in the Irish Sea near the Isle of Man.

Above: A party in the bow torpedo compartment after the commissioning of *U1024* in August 1944.

Right: Men at the party after the commissioning of *U1024*. Several authors have told us that men were apparently forced to serve in U-boats, but do these faces really look like people under such pressure?

Gutteck lacked in experience, he made up with determination and continuously pressed forward towards convoys. Schnorkelling at night without surfacing had the great disadvantage of easily disorientating navigators because they were less likely to notice good, clear opportunities for taking sights on the stars. *U1024* did have the advantage of obtaining excellent bearings on a number of lights along the Irish coast before starting aggressive action, but soon afterwards a grey veil of fog reduced visibility to less than 500m, causing a dramatic deterioration in the situation.

The fact that there were no longer lookouts on the top of the conning tower did not hamper the process of finding the enemy. Instead *U1024* used the sensitive and sophisticated sound detection gear which could almost always hear ships at far greater distances than they could ever be seen from the conning tower. The main problem was that the number and determination of the hunters meant it was now impractical to surface for bursts of fast speed to manoeuvre in front of any merchant ships that might be detected. Instead *U1024* had to move slowly, relying mainly on the inadequate performance of its electric motors. Masses of confusing noises were eventually responsible for bringing down the crew's morale. Unable to see what was causing them, the men were at the mercy of a wild orchestra of terrifying sounds with contributions from a variety of different engines and propellers and Asdic, all of which helped in adding a highly frightening sequence of reverberations from which there was no escape.

The men in the central control room were experiencing life-threatening situations they had hardly been told about. Unable to take long rests, Gutteck was required to make quick decisions to extract his boat from one agonising predicament after another. Yet, he escaped several times, leaving his hunters to work out their fury on wrecks or rocks in the shallow waters. He even had the good fortune of being able to raise his schnorkel on several occasions to ventilate the interior and, at other times, to run the diesels for brief periods for recharging the batteries, though another disadvantage with schnorkelling was that the noisy diesels rendered the sound detection gear useless and the engines had to be switched off at regular intervals to check that nothing was creeping up. There was a radar detection aerial on the top of the schnorkel head, but this would only work as long as the enemy was using his electronics. There was no way of detecting approaching aircraft or ships with their radar switched off. Of course, both periscopes were raised as well, but it could well be too late by the time anything was spotted through them in the blackness of the night.

Twisting out of the way of approaching ships, being lashed by pings and squeaks and shattered by detonations made for a nerve-wracking few days. The waters were so shallow that even the bombs from the anti-submarine mortars, designed to explode only on contact, hit the bottom to go off with deafening roars. Although not fatal, the noise still smashed the nerves of the men confined inside their cramped iron hull. Finally, the end came quite quickly from a well-placed detonation. Lights went out, machinery was ripped from the walls, men were stunned and water started pouring into the diesel compartment so fast that even the watertight doors could not be opened briefly to inspect the damage. There was nothing the men could do. The boat was out of control. Gutteck gave the order to prepare for abandoning ship and *U1024* surfaced into a hail of gunfire. Clambering up on to the bridge, Gutteck had one of his arms shot away. German records say that he was killed by enemy gunfire, but British records state that he pulled a pistol from his coat and shot himself. Whatever may be the truth, he died leaving his men in unrehearsed confusion, to make the best out of what could be their last minutes on earth.

The frigate HMS *Loch Glendhu* (Lt-Cdr E. G. P. B. Knapton), responsible for bringing the U-boat to the surface, opened fire immediately when it appeared above the waves, but it quickly became apparent that the men staggering out on to the upper deck were at the end of their tether and in no position to retaliate. The frigate *Loch More* (Lt-Cdr R. A. D. Cambridge) closed in and scrambled her boarding party. The secrets from the interior were quickly and systematically removed while, at the same time, other men attached a hawser with a view to towing the U-boat to harbour. Unfortunately for the Royal Navy, there was too much water in the aft section, which later pulled *U1024* into the depths of the Irish Sea. The hoard of secret material was as impressive as the material captured from *U110*, but of limited use. The war in Europe ended less than four weeks later and soon after that the British had more surrendered U-boats than they knew what to do with.

Above: Men from *U1024* on deck. A good number of historians have claimed that U-boat men got younger as the war progressed, although statistics show the exact opposite. *U1024* was commissioned some eight months before the end of the war and these men don't look to be terribly young.

Above: U243 at sea, showing the type of hinged schnorkel carried by *U1024* when it was captured. The raising mechanism of the rigid air pipe, protruding above the deck, lifted the schnorkel until it could be locked into the bracket at the top of the conning tower.

Top left: A schnorkel in the raised position. The exhaust duct around the outside of the tower, running up from the diesel compartment, was later placed inside the fairing of some boats. The two triangles painted on the side of the tower are an identification symbol for training, suggesting that the boat is due to go on trials and the wooden strips of camouflage over the deck indicate that this photograph was probably taken while the boat was still lying at the builder's yard.

Below left: A rigid schnorkel lying in the deck casing of a Type VIIC.

Right: The head valve with ball float on the top and the diesel exhaust towards the bottom of the picture. The head has been covered with soft rubber to absorb radar impulses. The circular dipole aerial on the top is a radar detector.

Below: Engineering officer Nagel, Watch Officer Lange and Chief Mechanic Wehling on the bridge of *U260*. The special pressure-resistant binoculars can be seen clipped ready in position on top of the torpedo aimer. On the right is the blurred image of the partly raised attack periscope.

Above: The sequoia, which has often been erroneously referred to as a cedar, and the mansion at Bletchley Park. The original crown of this tree was brought down during a storm, but before the war it acted as a mast for the aerial of the famous Radio Station X.

Chapter 15
Bletchley Park and the British Side

Names

Before the war, deciphering secret codes was carried out by the Government Code and Cipher School or GC&CS at Bletchley Park. The information this organisation produced was known as Special Intelligence and code-named Ultra, but even those terms were used as little as possible in order to preserve secrecy. Instead the origins were attributed to a variety of other sources, many of them fictitious.

Before the war, there was also a radio listening station in the water tower at Bletchley Park. Its name, Station Ten, is nearly always written with a Roman numeral, hence the by now famous term of Station X. To prevent sinking into a sea of confusing names, 'Bletchley Park' is used throughout this book.

The Park

The 55 fenced and walled acres of Bletchley Park were vacated shortly after the war and everything within it removed, leaving only a mass of empty buildings. Since this order of total destruction came directly from the highest sources, the process was especially thorough. Nothing was left in situ. Consequently, some of the century's most fascinating pieces of technology and incredible innovation were destroyed.

The term 'innovation' has a special meaning at Bletchley Park and to appreciate it fully one needs to take a conducted tour around the estate. The technology there was stunning. It ranged from the world's first programmable computer, years ahead of its time, to an ingenious shuttle system for passing secrets from one hut to another without the papers getting wet. This was done with the aid of a small tunnel connecting Hut 6 and Hut 3. Inside was a box with a piece of string attached to each end. A broom handle was rattled inside the tunnel as a signal for someone at the other side to pull the box. These days this might be regarded as a joke, but it has been reported here to illustrate the unbelievable simplicity with which much of the work was done. People worked in austere and at times even appallingly uncomfortable conditions, often with only the simplest of aids. It was brain power, patience, perseverance, making do and determination which produced the extraordinary results. Sophistication and innovation were only a small part of the overall job.

At Bletchley Park the word 'hut' has rather a special meaning. Some of the original wooden shacks, which gave rise to this term, are still standing and so are the majority of the brick-built 'huts'. Long after the war, a demolition contractor discovered that rather special meaning the hard way. This happened when British Telecom, who had purchased the site, decided to remove a number of the unwanted buildings and an expert demolition firm agreed to complete the apparently simple task in four weeks. Imagine everybody's surprise when the heavy breaking gear arrived, started working and was promptly wrecked by the buildings it was trying to knock down. The cloak of secrecy still hanging over the place meant no one knew the apparently dilapidated buildings had been designed to resist something more powerful than a crane with an iron ball hanging at the end. That frail-looking, almost shoddy construction had been put there to withstand near-misses from heavy bomb blasts. Removing it was going to do more than challenge the average demolition expert. The four-week job turned into a four-month-long undertaking and then British Telecom decided it would be better to leave the other stubborn bunkers where they were.

The blast-proof construction was never put to the test. Only once throughout the entire war did bombs fall within the boundaries of the Park and even then, it appears probable that the nearby railway sidings were the target rather than the conglomeration of huts. The Bletchley railway complex resembled a nearby industrial area and since there was only one solitary bomber it is probable that he was searching for something more interesting than a country house with huts around a lake. This one bombing, on 20 November 1940, hardly created a disturbance and no significant damage. One bomb fell close to Hut 4, where naval intelligence was processed, and another demolished a derelict greenhouse, but the heating system from this had already been moved to one of the early huts, so no one was terribly worried. Bletchley Park was left in peace for the remainder of the war.

Immediately after the war an acute shortage of accommodation of all types meant that maximum use had to be squeezed out of all buildings, including the empty complex at Bletchley Park. It was used successively as a teacher training college, for schooling telephone engineers and as a school for civil aviation ground staff before the antiquated facilities fell, once more, into disuse. Local people took advantage of the neglect by enjoying walks through the grounds and feeding ducks on the pond. By the 1990s Bletchley Park had been surrounded by a mass of new housing and it was decided to demolish the ageing and decaying remnants with a view to turning the area into a respectable part of Milton Keynes new town. At this critical stage, with

Above: During the war the huts at Bletchley Park were surrounded by bomb blast protection walls, making the interiors quite dim. This shows Ellen Spark, a former Wren who worked at Bletchley, sitting on the remains of these old walls.

bulldozers poised to move in, the Bletchley Park Trust was formed to make some attempts at conserving what is a major part of the nation's heritage.

It would seem that code breaking at Bletchley Park in fact started some time before the war. At first a long wire was hung from the mansion's water tower to a sequoia tree on the front lawn and back again as an aerial for making the first attempts at intercepting foreign radio transmissions. (Actually that tree has often been named as a cedar, which shows that cryptanalysts make poor botanists.) In those days it was a case of picking up the right signals on the correct frequency at the precise time. When the war started it was realised that this huge spider's web of wire was a dead give-away and it was quickly dismantled. At the same time listening stations were duplicated and moved away to other nearby locations, while Bletchley Park concentrated on trying to make sense of the intercepted messages. This was a daunting task, but the experts quickly realised that they could glean considerable information from the general appearance of the jumbled letters without knowing the precise meaning of the messages. This knowledge was often supplemented with bearings from radio direction finders, making it possible to guess where the activity was taking place. These radio direction finding stations are an enigma in themselves. Being highly secret as well, it is difficult to determine how many there actually were, but recent research would suggest there were at least 48 of them.

This detective work of sifting through piles of meaningless letters had hardly been done before. When the war started, amateur spies disguised in dirty raincoats with sunglasses and carrying small quantities of information in cunningly concealed places were still a reality. Never before had such vast volumes of meaningless text built up in one place. Consequently, hardly anything at Bletchley Park could be designed. There was no rule book and no one to call upon for advice. Things just happened. And things happened wherever a space could be found for them to take place. Hut 4, for example, where naval intelligence was evaluated, was literally plonked on flower beds right in front of the mansion's windows. A few slabs were laid down with brick piers and the hut erected on top. There was no time for sophistication, planning or proper building. It was a case of 'can we please have it as soon as possible or earlier'. This mushrooming of huts and facilities was made even worse by Bletchley Park's early modest success. Prime Minister Churchill could see that something big and wonderful was growing there and gave the Park whatever it needed but there was no one who knew very far in advance what Bletchley Park did require. Nobody knew what they wanted until they needed it and then it was required in a great hurry.

A close look at the mansion will show that such a way of working was apt in a sense. The original house had been built along very much the same lines. A bit was added whenever more space was needed, without much

Above: Looking across the driveway towards Hut 11, which used to house the bombes, mechanical computers for decrypting the Enigma codes. A Wren employed in the hut behind this building said that she walked along the path by the cycle shed for every working day of the war and never knew what went on inside. Those operating the bombes inside found conditions very trying. The machines generated a great deal of heat, meaning the people were always subjected to an almost unbearably stuffy atmosphere.

Left: The skylight of Hut 11, showing the thickness of the reinforced ceiling. A good number of windows and virtually all the skylights were postwar additions, put in when the buildings were used for educational purposes.

regard to style or consideration of what was already there. As a result, the mansion grew in a hotchpotch fashion, almost as if the builder incorporated every suggestion from a committee representing vastly varying interests.

It has already been said in the first chapter that the original Bletchley Park was self-sufficient, with its own water supply, electricity generators, vegetable gardens and so on, and this had to be further developed once the GC&CS moved there. Too much might be destroyed by the time the village fire engine arrived and imagine the security risk if a fireman saw something in one of the huts before it became general knowledge. Secrecy had to be preserved. Outsiders could not be allowed in under any circumstances. A general atmosphere of secrecy swept through the land and at Bletchley Park it became an even greater necessity of daily life. So much so that parts of the Park were isolated from others and everybody who worked there in any capacity had to sign the Official Secrets Act. The Park also needed its own domestic services such as fire brigade, maintenance engineers and so forth.

Most of the raw information arrived at Bletchley Park by dispatch riders or through telex lines in the form of unintelligible intercepted messages in Enigma code. These were then deciphered and rewritten in words. This was important because in the original there were just jumbles of letters without gaps in the right places. This readable data was then passed to an intelligence hut where it was evaluated and transmitted to the correct places. Very few sea-going officers would have known about Bletchley Park. Only the commanding officers of major units and one or two of their staff would have had any knowledge of Ultra. Apart from this tight circle, only the officer responsible for receiving and distributing the messages at each land headquarters would have known what was being handled or where it came from. At the headquarters of the Western Approaches Command in Liverpool, the terminal from Bletchley Park was accommodated in a small room, about three metres square, with telex machine and telephone. The operator locked himself in to prevent intrusions and, on top of this, an armed guard was posted outside the door. And all this inside a huge top secret, guarded bunker with three-metre-thick walls and a ceiling of more than half a metre of reinforced concrete.

Much of the information which flowed into Bletchley Park was of no immediate operational use until the snippets of knowledge could be correlated with other seemingly valueless intercepts. None of this, however, could have been of any benefit if could not be retrieved when required. This was done by creating an index with post-card-sized cards, many of them stored initially in nothing more permanent than shoe boxes. The snag was that Bletchley Park required more boxes than there were new shoes in the area and something stronger had to be specially ordered. This build-up of information soon grew into massive proportions. By the end of the war it was

Above: Many of the windows at Bletchley Park were hidden behind blast protection walls, making it impossible for a passer-by to peep through the glass. This shows one of the original windows at Bletchley Park with one-way mirror glass, making it exceedingly difficult to see the interior from the outside even where there was no wall.

housed in a purpose-built 'hut', big enough comfortably to accommodate a good sized school. This was of such immense value that Britain often knew more about German dispositions than German commanders in the field. In addition to this, Bletchley Park often decoded messages and delivered them for appropriate action before those vital details reached their German destination. A truly remarkable achievement.

The aim of the Bletchley Park Trust is to create a memorial to cryptography, intelligence work and computing by building up what hopefully will become one of the major heritage sites in southern England. There are facilities for accommodating a large number of individual groups such as The Churchill Collection, an aircraft recovery group, a model boat club, model railway society, a uniform and memorabilia collection, a radio club, a German signals command post, a computing display, a vehicle restoration group, a display showing the wartime fire fighting services, the Oxford Squadron RAAF, RAF history, the Parachute Regiment Association, Light Infantry history, post office, US re-enactment group and many more. In future it is hoped also to have a detailed exhibition showing other aspects of World War 2 such as the Battle of the Atlantic, convoys and various appropriate aspects of the German armed forces. In addition to these permanent displays, the grounds are also used throughout the year for various temporary gatherings, including a military vehicle weekend, radio meetings, reunions and so forth. For anyone interested in finding out details of open days, there is a special telephone information line: 01908 640404.

Above: Bletchley Park's fire engines in their garage waiting for a call that hardly ever came. Luckily for the cryptanalysts the Park was bombed only once throughout the whole war. The object on the extreme right is a bucket with stirrup pump. This was similar to the pumps used to inflate tyres, except that it squirted water. This standard equipment was common throughout the war.

Above: The side gate at Bletchley Park with sentry box behind the wall on the left. One of the bombs which fell in the Park landed on the right and caused a little damage to the Naval Intelligence Hut 4 beyond the trees.

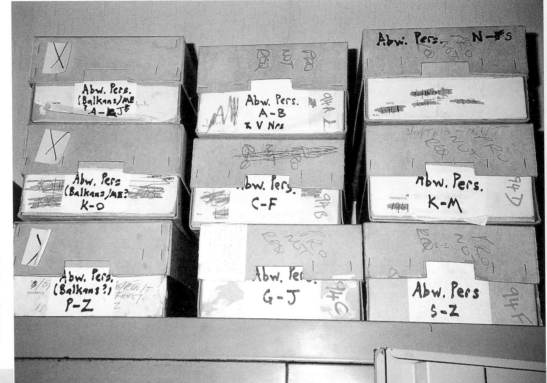

Right: The last remains of the massive card index at Bletchley Park. Cards were stored in these stout cardboard boxes.

Below: The side of the building where the card index was accommodated throughout the war years. This was big enough to house a modern school and a large number of people worked there constantly filing and sorting information.

Left: The Colossus rebuild now on display at Bletchley Park. Very little of the original machine survived and it has been re-created by a small team of dedicated experts piecing together whatever operators could remember. The fact that this has been done is almost as great an achievement as building the original. Colossus was the world's first programmable electronic computer, whose switching mechanism was based on radio valves rather than transistors.

Right: A reconstructed radio listening station at Bletchley Park, showing the type of room where operators listened in on German U-boat transmissions.

Left: The type of radio used to intercept U-boat radio messages. Operators would usually wear the heavy headsets and spend their working time writing down chains of meaningless letters. This tedious work would have been common to both sides because the majority of operators in land stations would not have known the meanings of the messages they were handling. Despite the incredibly stressful atmosphere, some British operators noticed mistakes being made by the other side and highlighted those sections for the cryptanalysts.

Above and below: Among the numerous displays at Bletchley Park is a magnificent collection of model ships. These pictures show two corvettes, the type of ship developed for hunting U-boats.

Above: Members of the 146 Pioniers, a World War 2 re-enactment group at Bletchley Park during the annual Military Vehicles Weekend.

Above: A scene from World War 2 re-created at Bletchley Park for the annual Military Vehicles Weekend.

Right: Decrypted U-boat signals from Bletchley Park ended up in the cellar below this building still standing close to Admiralty Arch in London. There Commander Rodger Winn worked with a dedicated team to evaluate the meaning of the masses of information flooding in. Known as the Citadel, the massive concrete bunker is hidden behind the green vines now covering the eyesore.

Below: The Mall in London, with Admiralty Arch immediately behind the camera and Buckingham Palace in the distance, showing the location of the Citadel where the secret British U-boat Tracking Room was housed.

Right: The front of Derby House in Liverpool with the headquarters of the Western Approaches Command in its cellar, which controlled the convoys crossing the Atlantic. This was another grateful recipient for decrypted U-boat messages from Bletchley Park.

Below: Huts at Bletchley Park in 1948 after the bomb blast protection walls had been taken down and the buildings were being used as a college of education for training teachers. The students have built a model of a lock in the Grand Union Canal in what had been an open water tank. This was located on the roundabout, which is still there. Mrs G. Calcutt, one of the first students there, said that conditions were quite primitive because the facilities had not been used for some time and there was even brown water coming out of the plumbing system.

Above: The refectory for the college of education at Bletchley Park in 1948, showing the interior of the famous huts. The bomb blast protection walls during the war would have considerably reduced the amount of light shining in through the windows. No doubt the Wrens would have eaten their meals under very similar conditions.

Right: One of the last signals sent through the Enigma code. This is the order not to scuttle ships nor destroy military and civilian instalations.

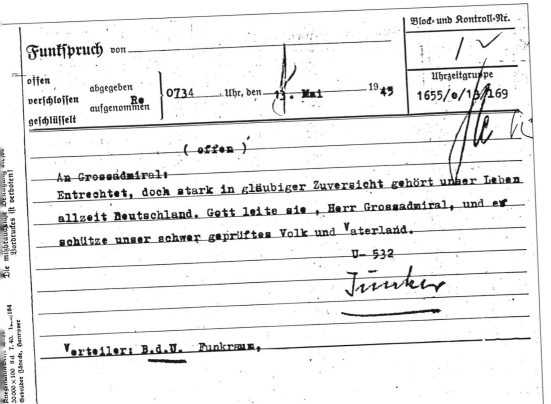

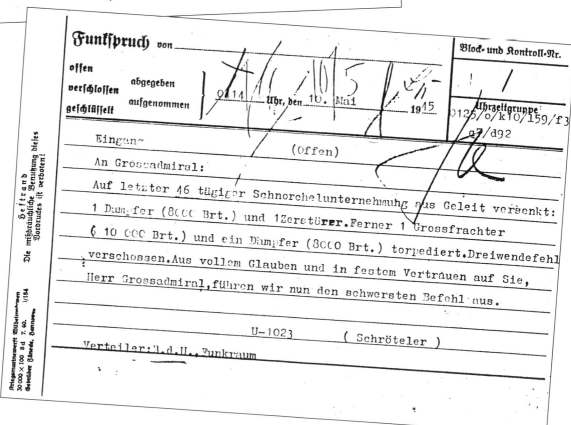

This page: Two of the last radio transmissions to be received by the U-boat Command in Enigma code before the end of the war. Translations are as follows: *(Left)* 'Deprived of our rights but still with strong faithful trust our lives will always belong to Germany. May God guide you and protect our deeply tried people. *U532* (signed) Ottoheinrich Junker' *(Below)* 'During our recent 16-day long schnorkel operation we sunk one ship (8000 GRT) and one destroyer in a convoy. In addition to this we torpedoed one large freighter (10,000 GRT). With faithful confidence we shall now carry out the most difficult order. *U1023* Schröteler'

Chapter 16
The Enigma Machine

Above: An Enigma machine, showing: (1) the plug board, (2) the keyboard and (3) the lamps which illuminate when a key is pressed. Above (or to the right of) the lamps are the three rotors used in this design. Some Enigma machines could be locked with a key and also had a socket to connect an external 6-volt power supply. This machine has a switch to the right of the rotors, with a facility for testing the light bulbs.

Right: A front view of a three-wheel Enigma machine, showing a good number of plugs in position.

Left: A close-up of the plug board.

Below: A close-up of a four-rotor Enigma machine, with the cover hinged up, on display at Bletchley Park.

Above: A dismantled Enigma wheel on display at Bletchley Park. From left to right: (1) the casing with notched wheel which could be rotated to fit into any one of the 26 possible positions; (2) a metal rim which fitted inside the notched wheel; (3) a black plate with 26 flat contacts on the left wired to 26 spring-loaded pins on the right.

Above: An end-on view of an Enigma rotor showing the flat plate contacts on one side.

Above: The spring-loaded pins which brushed against flat contacts on the other side of the rotor. A lever pushed against the black notches to turn the right-hand wheel one position every time a key was pressed. Once the wheel had gone through a complete rotation, the next wheel was moved one notch along to provide a different set of combinations.

Grabbing the Enigma: Occasions Where Allied Forces Boarded German Vessels

1939

3 September
The British destroyer *Somali* (Capt Nicholson) captured the German freighter *Hannah Böge* to the south of Iceland, making this the first German ship to fall into Allied hands.

1940

12 February
U33 (Kptlt Hans-Wilhelm von Dresky) was sunk by HMS *Gleaner* (Lt-Cdr H. P. Price) in the Clyde estuary (Scotland) and several rotors from the Enigma machine were captured. Following this, Royal Navy divers tried diving on the wreck with the hope of recovering the machine. Cold temperatures, strong currents and relatively deep water made this a dangerous undertaking.

16 February
The supply ship *Altmark* (Kpt Dau) was boarded inside a Norwegian fjord by men from the destroyer HMS *Cossack*.

15 April
U49 (Kptlt Curt von Gossler) was sunk in Vaags Fjord by HMS *Fearless* (Cdr K. Harkness) and HMS *Brazen* (Lt-Cdr M. Culme-Seymour). A number of secret documents, showing U-boat dispositions, floated to the surface to be collected by the Royal Navy.

26 April
Patrol boat (Vorpostenboot) *V2623* was captured by the Royal Navy.

1941

3/4 March
The patrol boat *Krebs* was captured during the British commando raid on the Lofoten Islands (Norway) and some secret material was captured. The destroyer *Somali* put her out of action and recovered sufficient material for Bletchley Park to read part of the German radio code for parts of March and April.

7 May
The weather ship *München*, a converted trawler, was captured by a British hunting force. The destroyer *Somali* (Capt Caslon) went alongside to capture secret documents. This material was sent to Britain aboard the destroyer HMS *Nestor* and enabled Bletchley Park to read some of the German radio codes until June.

9 May
U110 (Kptlt Fritz-Julius Lemp) was brought to the surface by depth charges from HMS *Aubrietia* (Lt-Cdr V. F. Smith) while HMS *Bulldog* (Cdr A. J. Baker-Cresswell) went on a ramming course. Realising that a capture might come off, he stopped and the ships succeeded in capturing the U-boat without the survivors being aware that their boat did not sink. A great deal of valuable material was recovered.

4 June
The supply tanker *Gedania* for battleship *Bismarck* and heavy cruiser *Prinz Eugen* was captured by the British auxiliary cruiser HMS *Marsdale*.

15 June
The supply tanker *Lothringen* for battleship *Bismarck* and heavy cruiser *Prinz Eugen* was captured by the cruiser HMS *Dunedin* and aircraft from the carrier HMS *Eagle*.

28 June
The weather ship *Lauenburg* was discovered by the destroyer HMS *Bedouin*, part of a Royal Navy hunting force. The destroyer *Tartar* went alongside to recover a variety of secret documents. This enabled Bletchley Park to read some of the German radio messages until the end of July.

27 August
U570 (Kptlt Hans-Joachim Rahmlow) surrendered to an aircraft, Hudson 'S', from RAF Squadron No 269 (Sqn Ldr J. H. Thompson) and was later moved to Britain to be commissioned as HMS *Graph*. It would appear that

much of the interior was smashed by the crew before the Royal Navy came on board and therefore it seems likely, according to German reports, that the Enigma machine and code books were thrown overboard.

10 September

U501 (Kptlt Hugo Förster) was attacked by escorts from convoy SC42. The corvette HMCS *Chambly* (Cdr J. S. Prentice) made the first contact and dropped depth charges. These brought *U501* to the surface right alongside another corvette, HMCS *Moosejaw* (Lt F. E. Grubb), so that Förster managed to step from the conning tower on to the deck of his attacker. Following this there was considerable confusion, but men from the Royal Navy succeeded in getting inside the U-boat before it went down, taking with it Stoker W. Brown from the boarding party into the depths.

1942

30 October

U559 (Kptlt Hans Heidtmann) was brought to surface in the Mediterranean near Port Said under rather dramatic circumstances and boarded by men from HMS *Pakenham* (Capt E. K. B. Stevens) who succeeded in salvaging valuable material. This enabled Bletchley Park to break into the new four-wheel radio code.

1943

17 February

U205 (ObltzS Friedrich Bürgel) was boarded by men from the destroyer HMS *Paladin* (Lt E. Bailey) and numerous items were captured. The submarine was taken in tow by HMS *Gloxinia* with a view of beaching it in North Africa but it sank in deep water a short distance from the coast.

17 April

U175 (Kptlt Heinrich Bruns) was brought to the surface during the battle with the US coastguard cutters *Spencer* and *Duane* amidst considerable confusion during which a merchant ship from convoy HX233 hit *Spencer* with a shell from a 5in gun. A number of Americans boarded the U-boat before it sank, but they claimed not to have salvaged anything.

12 September

U617 (Kptlt Albrecht Brandi) was stranded in North Africa near Melilla of neutral Spanish Morocco. It is possible but not likely that Britain violated neutrality to board the boat.

1944

6 March

U744 (ObltzS Heinz Blischke) was brought to the surface a short distance ahead of *Chilliwack* (Lt-Cdr G. R. Coughlin) and, seeing that there was an opportunity of a capture, other ships from the escort group raced over to get men on board the U-boat. The escort group from convoy HX280 consisted of HMS *Icarus*, HMS *Kenilworth Castle*, HMCS *St Catherines*, HMCS *Chaudière*, HMCS *Gatineau* and HMCS *Fennel*.

3 May

U852 (Kptlt Heinz-Wilhelm Eck) was beached in Somalia (East Africa) and the Royal Navy boarded the wreck, which was lying above water at low tide. The hull was drilled to establish the thickness of the metal and some documents, including the log, were recovered, but it seems likely that both the Enigma machine and the documentation for it had been thrown overboard in deep water before the boat was beached.

4 June

U505 (ObltzS Harald Lange) was captured by the aircraft carrier USS *Guadalcanal* off Dakar (Africa) and towed across the Atlantic to be commissioned as USS *Nemo*. Later, in 1954, the boat was moved to become an exhibit at the Science and Industry Museum in Chicago.

1945

13 April

U1024 (Kptlt Hans-Joachim Gutteck) was forced to the surface in the Irish Sea near the Isle of Man and taken in tow by HMS *Loch More* (Lt-Cdr R. A. D. Cambridge), but the U-boat went down during the following night.

Appendix II
Captured U-boats

The Boats, Their Types, Launching Dates & Builders (In chronological order of having been boarded or captured)

BOAT	TYPE	LAUNCHED DAY	MONTH	YEAR	LOCATION	BUILDER
U33	VIIA	11	June	1936	Kiel	Krupp Germania Works
U49	VIIB	24	June	1939	Kiel	Krupp Germania Works
U110	IXB	25	August	1940	Bremen	Deschimag AG Weser
U570	VIIC	20	March	1941	Hamburg	Blohm und Voss
U501	IXC/40	25	January	1941	Hamburg	Deutsche Werft
U559	VIIC	8	January	1941	Hamburg	Blohm und Voss
U205	VIIC	20	March	1941	Kiel	Krupp Germania Works
U175	IXC	2	September	1941	Bremen	Deschimag AG Weser
U744	VIIC	11	March	1943	Danzig	Schichau Works
U852	IXD2	28	January	1943	Bremen	Deschimag AG Weser
U505	IXC/40	24	May	1941	Hamburg	Deutsche Werft
U250	VIIC	11	November	1943	Kiel	Krupp Germania Works
U1024	VIIC	3	May	1944	Hamburg	Blohm und Voss

Type VII was a single-hull design based on UBIII of World War 1 and a prototype built in Finland under the name of *Vetehinen*, which was extensively tested by German technicians. Production of the resulting design started early in 1935 simultaneously at Deschimag in Bremen and Germania Works in Kiel. The first launch of a Type VII (*U33*) took place in Kiel on 11 June 1936, followed a fortnight later by *U27*, in Bremen. One wonders how much voluntary sweat and overtime went into these efforts to be the first yard to get these boats to water. Although originally classed as 'sea-going' (rather than shorter-range 'coastal' or longer-range 'ocean-going' types), these relatively small but sturdy boats could reach the American side of the Atlantic. With well over 600 eventually going into production, the Type VII has gained a place in the record books as the largest submarine class ever to be built.

Modifications of the original design were already in hand by the time the first boat was launched, but the improved version, Type VIIB, was not laid down until a few years later, after boats had been thoroughly tested. A further improvement, Type VIIC, followed exceedingly quickly, with the first 'C' series sliding off the stocks at a time when other yards were still adding the finishing touches to their VIIBs.

Type IX differed inasmuch that it was double-hulled, based on the design of *U81* of World War 1. This meant that the pressure hull, which resisted high water forces when diving, was surrounded by a multitude of tanks. Whether these contained air or liquids, their bottoms were always open to the sea, allowing water in and out, to equalise the pressure. The presence of these tanks allowed a considerably wider deck to be fitted above the top of the pressure hull and for more fuel to be carried.

Type IX also went through phases of being modified from series A, to B and then C. Later versions of both VIIC and IXC were strengthened for deeper diving and slightly improved to meet the changing demands of war. Each of these variations was identified by the year of conception, such as C/40, C/42, etc.

The larger, ocean-going Type IX was originally conceived as a mobile command centre to accommodate a tactical commander at sea, together with his small staff. However, these plans never materialised and the basic design was further developed as a long-range boat (Type IXD1 and IXD2), some of which later made monumental voyages to the Far East.

Sm or sea mile has been used as the abbreviation for nautical mile in the following tables because it best matches the original German *Seemeile*. Comparative distances are as follows:

	SEA MILE	LAND MILE	KILOMETRE
Sea mile	1	1.15	1.85
Land mile	0.87	1	1.61
Kilometre	0.54	0.62	1

Above: Deschimag AG Weser in 1999 during the final stages of demolition. The fitting out bays of Germany's largest shipbuilder were once located along this quayside. The low building in the distance with the large windows is situated on top of the old slipways where so many famous U-boats were assembled. *U110* and many more sailed for the first time from here. Today the site resembles a vast empty desert awaiting redevelopment.

Technical Data

		VIIA	VIIB	VIIC	IXB	IXC
Displacement:	Surface	626t	753t	769t	1051t	1120t
	Submerged	915t	1040t	1070t+	1408t	1540t
Length		64.5m	66.5m	66.5m	76.5m	76.5m
Beam		5.9m	6.2m	6.2m	6.5m	6.5m
Depth (diameter of pressure hull)		4.4m	4.7m	4.7m	4.7m	4.7m
Speed (maximum surface)		16kt	17kt	17kt	18kt	18kt
(cruising surface)		10kt	10kt	10kt	10kt	10kt
Speed (maximum submerged)		8kt	8kt	7.6kt	7.3kt	7.3kt
(cruising submerged)		4kt	4kt	4kt	4kt	4kt
Radius of Action:	high speed	2900sm	3250sm	5050sm	3800sm	5000sm
	cruising speed	6200sm	8500sm	11200sm	12000sm	13450sm
	most economical speed	6800sm	9500sm	13000sm	12400sm	16300sm
	Submerged	95sm	90sm	80sm	64sm	63sm
Maximum Diving Depth		200m	200m	250m	200m	200m
Diving Time:	Stationary	50sec	50sec	50sec	65sec+	65sec+
	Alarm dive/moving	30sec	30sec	30sec	35sec	35sec

Displacement

There were small variations in the displacements of these types. Therefore it is common to find a variety of slightly different figures. The majority of operational boats were modified throughout the war by enlarging conning towers, adding armour and anti-aircraft guns etc, all of which changed the basic configuration.

Speed and Radius of Action

One can quickly calculate that the cruising speed of a U-boat was roughly the same as a brisk cycling pace and even when boats were running at top speed, they could still have been overtaken by a cyclist. Once submerged, speed became even slower, and one can compare progress with walking, which could be increased to running speed for short periods during attacks or when evading the enemy.

It is virtually impossible to keep a submerged boat totally stationary because the balance is so delicate that it would either rise or sink very slowly. To overcome this problem, the Germans trimmed their boats on the heavy side and then maintained the required depth with the hydroplanes, which functioned in a similar manner to elevators on aircraft. Underwater, or perhaps to be more technically correct 'in the water', endurance was therefore always limited in part by the electricity in the batteries. Air for breathing also played a vital role, but during the first years of the war, it was rare for boats to remain submerged for longer than the hours of daylight and the problem of air purification only started playing a more significant role after the opposition became more determined. Then boats sometimes remained submerged for almost three days. Karl-Heinz Nitschke, the engineering officer of U377, has reported that on one occasion his readings of the carbon dioxide content in the boat showed that life should no longer be possible, yet everybody survived the ordeal.

Boats usually surfaced by adjusting the hydroplanes to glide up to periscope depth and then, if it was safe, rise higher to stick the top of the conning tower with air duct openings above the water. At this stage the diesel engines could be started so that exhaust fumes blew the water out of the diving tanks and thus bring the upper (outside) deck above the water. This last procedure could also be carried by blowing the tanks with compressed air. The storage bottles, looking like huge gas cylinders, were then refilled by an electric compressor, similar to the devices used for making compressed air for inflating car tyres in service stations.

In an emergency, perhaps when damage from depth charges resulted in water entering the interior, the whole boat could become too heavy for hydroplane control and the diving tanks would need to be blown with compressed air in this way. When this happened, boats arrived on the surface in a huge mass of bubbles and time was required before they could be made to submerge again (unless sufficient compressed air remained in the bottles so that these did not have to be refilled first). This period of time before diving again would be at least several minutes, long enough for a determined enemy to cripple the boat. Blowing the tanks deep down also had the great disadvantage that the air inside them expanded as water pressure reduced and thereby resulted in an uncontrollable increase in upwards motion as the boat rose through the water. These and other technicalities are explained in *The Underwater War 1939-1945* by Richard Compton-Hall, which is by far the best book on the subject.

Armaments

Torpedoes and Mines

Type VII had five and Type IX six torpedo tubes. In both cases there were four in the bows plus one or two in the stern. The Type VII has been recorded as carrying 14 torpedoes and the Type IX 22 torpedoes. These were stored in the smaller boat as follows:

One in each of the tubes	= 5
Two below the floor of the bow torpedo room	= 2
Four above the floor of the bow torpedo room	= 4
One under the floor of the rear compartment	= 1
Two in storage containers on the outside	= 2
Total:	= 14

Some boats had their tubes modified so that they could also eject torpedo mines, but not all commanders had the necessary training to lay them. There were two basic types of torpedo mine: Torpedo Mine Type B and Torpedo Mine Type C. The first mentioned was as long as half a torpedo and the other a third of the length. It is highly unlikely that a boat went to war armed only with mines and in the majority of minelaying cases they carried a mixture, usually with at least two torpedoes ready for shooting. The maximum number of mines which could be carried was about 39 in Type VII and 66 in Type IX. Each TMB mine was 2.31m long, weighed 740kg and had an external diameter of 53cm, the same as a torpedo.

Artillery

Type VII had one 88mm and Type IX one 105mm quick-firing deck gun just forward of the conning tower. The larger boat also carried a 37mm quick-firing gun on the after deck. None of these weapons had any sort of integral magazine; shells had to be fed singly into all these guns and ammunition was brought up from a locker below the radio room. A single 20mm anti-aircraft gun was usually also fitted either on or just aft of the conning tower. Later on in the war, the AA armament was increased quite dramatically. The common variations were two double 20mm guns and either one quadruple 20mm or a single 37mm anti-aircraft gun. This 37mm version varied from the deck gun by having a hopper for holding a number of shells for shooting in quick succession. U534, which is now being preserved in Birkenhead, has a most unusual 37mm twin AA gun on the rear platform, but this late introduction was rather rare.

Using guns at sea was quite tricky because the rocking boat made aiming difficult An artillery duel with even the smallest enemy surface warship would have been suicidal because one hit on the submarine could easily make it impossible to dive, while it was unlikely that a U-boat would have been able to hit a small, fast-moving target. So, U-boat guns were more often used against slow merchant ships which could not retaliate by shooting back.

Complement

Both basic Types VII and IX usually had four officers and 40-44 men, but these numbers were later increased to as many as 56 to man the additional anti-aircraft guns. In addition to this, it was quite likely that there would also be a trainee commander on board. On the other hand, boats sometimes went to sea with a few men missing when they fell ill or failed to return from leave in time.

The Internal Layout

Although Types VII and IX were two different classes, a boarder would hardly have noticed much difference. The appearance and internal layout was fairly similar. The hatches opening at upper deck level would usually not have been used at sea, therefore the only way in or out was through the conning tower. There was a hatch in the floor of the open bridge and another one at the base of the conning tower compartment, leading down into the central control room below it. In a Type VII the conning tower compartment housed the eyepieces of the attack periscope which was used by the commander during submerged actions. The eyepieces of the larger-headed sky or navigation periscope terminated inside the central control room, one deck lower down. The conning towers of the Type IX were large enough for both periscopes to fit into the upper, conning tower control room. A boarder would have found very little of value inside the conning tower. Even the important torpedo calculator or 'fruit machine' was screwed to the wall, making it exceedingly difficult to remove. Peering down from the hatch meant one's own body obscured much of the daylight, so that until his eyes became adjusted to the dim interior, a boarder would

The Boats, Their Commissioning Dates, Commanders and Date of Capture/Boarding

U33	25 July 1936	Ottoheinrich Junker	25 Jul 36 — 28 Oct 39
		Kurt Freiwald	22 Nov 36 — 20 Dec 36 and 3 Jun 37 — 25 Jul 37
		Hans-Wilhelm von Dresky	29 Oct 39 — 12 Feb 40
U49	12 August 1939	Curt von Gossler	15 Apr 40
U110	25 November 1940	Fritz-Julius Lemp	9 May 41
U570	15 May 1941	Hans-Joachim Rahmlow	27 Aug 41
U501	30 April 1941	Hugo Förster	10 Sep 41
U559	27 February 1941	Hans Heidtmann	30 Oct 42
U205	3 May 1941	Franz-Georg Reschke	until Oct 42
		Friedrich Bürgel	Oct 42 — 17 Feb 43
U175	5 December 1941	Heinrich Bruns	17 Apr 43
U744	5 June 1943	Heinz Blischke	6 Mar 44
U852	15 June 1943	Heinz-Wilhelm Eck	3 May 44
U505	26 August 1941	Axel-Olaf Loewe	5 Sep 42
		Peter Zschech*	6 Sep 42 — 24 Oct 43
		Paul Meyer	24 Oct 43 — 7 Nov 43
		Harald Lange	8 Nov 43 — 4 Jun 44
U250	12 December 1943	Werner-Karl Schmidt	30 Jun 44
U1024	28 June 1944	Hans-Joachim Gutteck	12 Apr 45

* Zschech committed suicide during a depth charge attack and the First Watch Officer, Paul Meyer, took command to bring the boat safely back to port.

Above: The machine shop at Deschimag AG Weser in Bremen still stands as one of the last remains of a once mighty shipbuilding empire. It is quite likely that parts of *U110* were assembled or finished off in this building. Railways played an important part in submarine construction because they brought in the majority of raw materials. The cobblestones of the road were of a relatively smooth variety usually found in built-up areas. Lorries and horse and carts could pass relatively easily over them without too many vibrations.

have been able to see little other than a vertical ladder surrounded by a mass of pipes and machinery, shrouding by dark nooks and crannies.

Climbing down into a rocking boat was not easy at the best of times and the bravery of boarders can hardly be described or imagined. Taking those few simple steps, was indeed an act of heroism which is difficult to comprehend today. There was always the risk that an injured crewman, unable to climb the ladder, remained below with sufficient energy to pull the trigger of a gun. The multitude of strange noises reverberating around the interior could have been timers of scuttling charges, waiting to blow the boat sky high. Furthermore, once inside, boarders had no way of knowing what was happening on the outside or seeing if the submarine was sinking.

Having reached the bottom of the ladder, boarders had to make a quick decision: turn either towards the bow or stern. This was made slightly easier in the larger Type IX because there was an engine room immediately aft of the central control room and the sight of oily machinery would probably have made intruders go the other way. Whichever way they went, they were faced with a small one-metre-diameter hatch in the pressure-resisting bulkhead. Going through the forward hatch, the boarders would have found the commander's 'cabin' to their left and the radio room on the right. This was where the richest pickings were to be had. Few significant papers or delicate instruments were kept in the central control room because when the boat was surfaced, even in moderate seas, a fair amount of

water would wash down the hatch, adding to the discomforts of this cramped space. There would have been charts with boat's course, but very little else.

Raiding the radio room could have produced a good haul, but a boarder, who was unlikely to know his way about, could just as well pick up a typewriter, a record player or radio for entertaining the crew rather than an Enigma machine. Among the supposedly secret papers, he could have grabbed a railway timetable for trains from home to base, the menu for the next two weeks, the latest rules for behaviour in the barracks back home or the secret key to work the radio. So, it was not just a case of grabbing what ever was lying around. However, it helped to know that official documents were usually bound in red covers.

Having grabbed this material, it had to be carried up a vertical ladder, and in case that sounds easy, just try doing it with one hand while holding a pile of books with the other. Then remember that in a rocking boat there are times when it appears as if you are hanging on the underside of the rungs. Even if you could carry them, there was no point in stuffing books under your arm and climbing up with them as it was not difficult to work out that the whole lot would fall apart as soon as they got wet. And the outside of the boat as well as the inside of the conning tower was pretty damp at the best of times. The physical effort of removing anything of value from a submarine was no mean feat and no medal will ever compensate for the bravery of those who managed it.

Above: During the early part of the 20th century, many German country roads were surfaced with irregular cobblestones, which made driving over them exceedingly irritating. Delicate instruments for submarines could easily have been damaged by the rough surface. This shows a lane close to the U-Boot-Archiv in Cuxhaven-Altenbruch still with its original surface which was laid at the turn of the century. Smooth, tarmac roads hardly existed until after the war and white painted road markings did not make an appearance until some fifteen years after the end of hostilities.

Above: River Weser in Bremen, looking towards the site where *U110* was launched in August 1940. This photograph was taken shortly after much of the shipyard had been demolished.

Above: The River Elbe in Hamburg during the early 1990s with the port's largest dry dock (Dock Elbe 17) in the background. This is part of the Blohm und Voss complex, which established itself as the most efficient submarine construction yard during the war.

Above: The majority of dry docks in Hamburg were of the floating variety as can be seen in this photograph. They could submerge for ships to float in and then the entire structure resurfaced to lift the vessel clear of the water. Many U-boats were finished off or repaired in these docks. The slipways where so many U-boats were built are still partly visible, tucked away behind this mass of floating docks.

Above: Krupp Germania Works in Kiel shortly before the site was redeveloped as the modern Scandinavian ferry terminal. The massive glass house which protected the U-boat slips used to stand on the far shore. This shipyard also built the German Navy's first U-boat, *U1*, in 1906.

Above: Krupp Germania Works in its heyday. The massive glass hangar, at that time probably the biggest such building in North Germany, was originally erected to provide protection for the building of sophisticated surface ships but military expansion and the war dictated that it should be used for sheltering submarines.

Above: This probably shows *U54*, a Type VIIB, on the stocks inside the massive glass hangar at Germania Works. *U49*, identical to this boat, was launched here just two months before this picture was taken. The large anchor was not part of the submarine's inventory but was carried for emergencies in case the boat gained too much momentum on launch and drifted over to the far shore.

Above: The launching of *U54* from inside the glass hangar at Krupp Germania Works. Although the site was often bombed by the Allied air forces, production continued throughout the war. The glass was blown out, but the metal frame remained until it was demolished after the war.

Above: Another Type VIIB being launched at Krupp Germania Works. Each yard had its own way of building and produced slightly different versions of the same design. This was especially noticeable in the locking mechanism of the hatches, where it is still possible to identify the builder by the layout of the mechanism. This fascinated the Royal Navy to such an extent after the war that experiments were carried out to find out which was the strongest by blowing open the hatches of captured boats.

Above: U69, the first Type VIIC to be launched, on the slipway at Germania Works. The saddle tank by the side of the conning tower can be seen as a well-defined bulge. It is strange that the net cutter was still being fitted to the bows as an anchorage for the jumping wire. They had been obsolete since World War 1 and even then there were hardly any situations where they were used.

Above: U573, a Type VIIC from Blohm und Voss in Hamburg, lying high in the water and clearly showing the vents along the side of the hull. The pressure hull, in which the crew and machinery were accommodated, is only just level with the surface of the water and what can be seen here was a casing built on top of it. The space between the upper deck and the pressure hull filled with water every time the boat dived and poured out of these vents when it surfaced again.

This page: U302 (Type VIIC) seen from a minesweeper alongside. This shows the early type of artillery, with an 88mm quick-firing gun forward of the conning tower and a single 20mm anti-aircraft gun on the Wintergarten ('Conservatory').

Left: Once in port, diving tanks were filled with air to lift the boats high out of the water so that the hatches in the pressure hull were well above the surface. At sea, boats were often trimmed lower for quicker diving. This shows the type of view a boarding party would have had as it approached a U-boat. This is *U200*, a long-distance Type IXD2 from Deschimag AG Weser. The rigid aerials for the boat's own radar system fixed to the front of the tower indicate that this picture was taken after aircraft started making a significant impact on the U-boat war, but before the anti-aircraft armament was strengthened.

Above: *U53*, a Type VIIB from Germania Works in Kiel, showing the early type of armament with 88mm quick-firing gun. The free flooding vents for allowing water into the space between the upper deck and the pressure hull can clearly be seen. The bronze eagles and the numbers on the conning tower were removed after the start of the war, making identification somewhat more difficult. The horseshoe-shaped object to the left of the number is a lifebelt, which was only attached to its bracket while the boat was manoeuvring in port. The hump at the base of the conning tower housed the magnetic compass, which could be viewed by the helmsman down below through an illuminated periscope.

Above: The 88mm quick-firing deck gun in action with crew wearing safety harnesses. The right-hand aimer rotated the gun while the man peering through the sights on the left adjusted the elevation. These two men could fire the gun by pressing the trigger.

Right: U165 (a Type IXC) with 105mm quick-firing gun. The 88mm and the 105mm guns looked fairly similar, but there was more deck space on the Type IX than on the smaller Type VII.

Above: The foredeck of *U755* (Type VIIC) with 88mm quick-firing gun and the T-shaped head of the sound detector. The hatch towards the left does not lead down into the boat, but is the lid of a pressure-resistant container. Emergency rescue buoys, ammunition or life-rafts were stored in these canisters.

Left: U165, a Type IXC, with 37mm quick-firing deck gun aft of the conning tower.

Right: U27, a Type VIIA, showing the early type of conning tower. This was a time when the navy had not yet thought of a possible threat from the sky and placed the mount for the 20mm anti-aircraft gun on the upper deck. This was impractical because it took a long time to carry the ammunition from below the radio room and that part of the deck was often particularly wet with waves washing around the base. The two holes to the left of the number are an intake for the radio aerial and a fog horn. The port navigation light can be seen to the right of the number, below the bracket for holding a horseshoe-shaped lifebuoy.

Above: Another view of the typical conning tower design before it was modified to meet the threat from the air.

Above: U71, a Type VIIC in Memel. This conning tower design has gone through considerable modification. The gun platform or Wintergarten has been enlarged to accommodate a single 20mm anti-aircraft gun and the upper lip or wind deflector has been changed to catch spray. Another spray deflector has been added half-way up the tower. The large black triangle on a white background is an identification mark applied during training and was used by a number of boats during their brief spell in the Baltic. Note that the boat in the foreground already has an additional lower gun platform but without armament which would suggest that this photograph was taken after the autumn of 1942.

Above: U764, a Type VIIC. The boat's upper structure has been modified to meet the threat from the air. This was done by removing the 88mm quick-firing gun forward of the conning tower, enlarging the upper gun platform to carry two 20mm twin anti-aircraft guns and by adding another, lower Wintergarten to hold a single 37mm anti-aircraft gun. The other common weapon on the lower platform was a 20mm quadruple. In later years even 37mm twins were made, but these were fitted to only very few of the bigger boats. This conning tower modification also reduced the underwater speed of the boats and the larger number of men up on deck meant diving took much longer.

Above: U677, a Type VIIC with the modified gun platforms, but photographed before all the artillery was installed. The hatch leading down to the galley can be seen to right of the conning tower.

Above: *U673*, a Type VIIC, still in pristine condition with the new enlarged Wintergarten behind the conning tower. The white triangle with a line above it is an identification for training. It is interesting to note that there are two jumping wires running down to the bows and only one at the stern. This modification was used briefly during the summer of 1943 to allow a fixed radar aerial to be operated from the front of the conning tower. The boat had to cruise in a circle in order to get a 360° sweep and a modified aerial was introduced by the autumn of 1943.

Left: *U251*, a Type VIIC, seen near Trondheim in Norway in 1943. This clearly shows how little space there was on the top of the conning tower. Note the signal lamp on the periscope support below the binoculars, and the brackets for holding the horseshoe-shaped lifebelt on the outside of the tower wall.

Left: This shows the typical narrow deck of a Type VII with huge saddle tanks on both sides of the hull.

Below: U43, a Type IXA, with ObltzS Paul-Karl Loeser on the left, the boat's medical officer Dr Pointer and Petty Officer Löhr on the right. Loeser later commanded *U373* and survived the war. Also on the right is the circular aerial of the radio direction finder which rotated and could be used to determine the direction from which radio signals were coming. Supply boats or those in contact with convoys could transmit signals for other boats to home in on. This was especially useful when bad weather made it difficult to get accurate bearings on the sun or stars.

Below: This probably shows *U43* under Kptlt Wilhelm Ambrosius, a double-hulled Type IXA with wide upper deck. The conning tower was also much bigger, but just as wet as on the smaller Type VIIs.

Right: U441 or *U440*, a Type VIIC. The white T-shaped head of the underwater sound detector has been turned lengthways on, but is still clearly visible. This was usually removed in port and therefore does not always feature in photographs. Behind it is the electric winch with capstan head so that it could be turned by muscle power in the event of a power failure. In front of this, the mooring rope has been attached to two retractable bollards.

Left: A close-up of the rear, above-deck torpedo tube of *U31*, a Type VIIA. This was the only type to have a torpedo tube outside the main hull.

Right: It is often difficult to distinguish between the Types VIIB and VIIC, but the stern of VIIA differed considerably by having a single torpedo tube mounted on the upper deck. This was not terribly successful because it had to be loaded from the outside and it could not be used to fire the fast G7a torpedoes in winter. These contained distilled water for a steam induced internal combustion engine, which often froze in cold weather. Although the 20mm gun has been removed from its mount, this picture clearly shows how difficult it must have been for the crew, if they had to engage a fast flying aircraft. Even if the men had managed to maintain a foothold on the slippery deck, they would have been buffeted by waves, making loading and aiming exceedingly difficult.

Above: Probably *U43*, a Type IXA, of which only eight were built before production was switched to the modified Type IXB. This, in turn, was revised after 14 boats and later 143 Type IXCs were commissioned.

Right: The conning tower of *U490*, a supply boat of Type XIV, under Kptlt Wilhelm Gerlach, who is peering through his binoculars towards the right. Britain could understand the German code by the time these massive submarines came into service and made a point of attacking U-boats at the vulnerable moment of being supplied. The gun forward of the conning tower was a small 37mm as defensive armament, although targets for this weapon hardly ever presented themselves and consequently they were seldom used.

Above: The 105mm quick-firing gun of *U172*, a Type IXC from Deschimag AG Weser in Bremen.

Right: The supply boat *U490* with men washing their smalls.

Below: The bows of a Type IX, probably *U43*, showing the T-shaped head of the underwater sound detection equipment in the foreground. Behind it is the winch and capstan head. Behind that is a red and white striped rescue buoy. This could be released from the inside of the boat and remained connected to it by a stout wire which also carried a telephone cable for emergencies. These buoys were later accommodated in containers with lids, but the war made them impractical and the device was discontinued. The thick lumps in the jumping wire running up to the top of the conning tower are insulators to prevent the aerial from earthing with the boat.

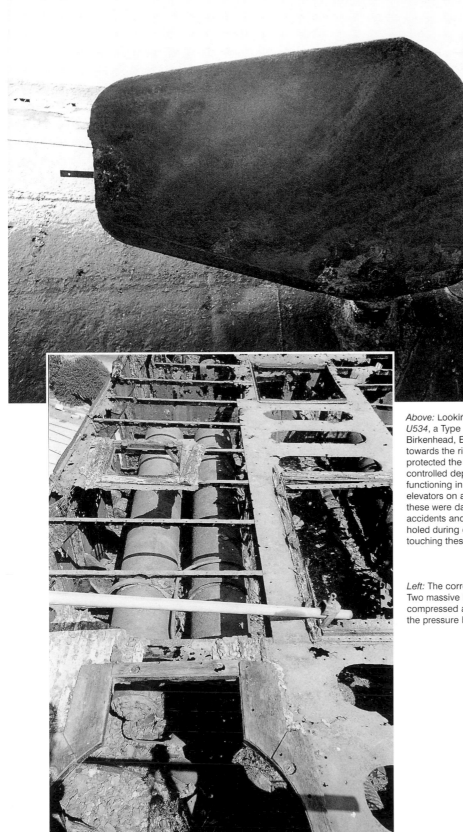

Above: Looking up at the hydroplane of *U534*, a Type IXC/40, now on display in Birkenhead, England. The narrow guard towards the right (and front of the boat) protected the blade. The hydroplanes controlled depth when submerged, functioning in a similar manner to elevators on aircraft. A good number of these were damaged during docking accidents and at least two escorts were holed during captures as a result of touching these structures.

Left: The corroded upper deck of *U534*. Two massive bottles for holding compressed air can be seen bolted to the pressure hull.

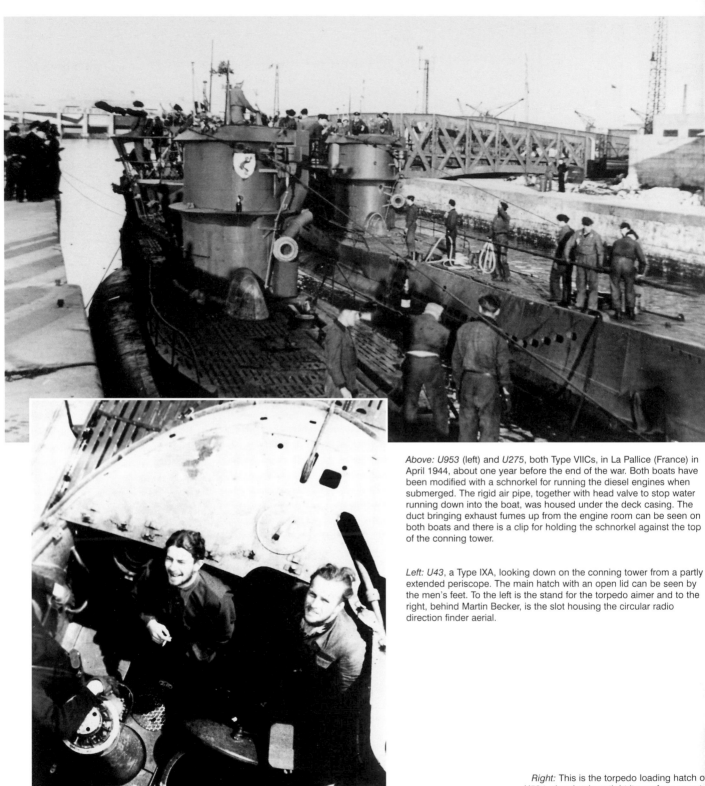

Above: U953 (left) and *U275*, both Type VIICs, in La Pallice (France) in April 1944, about one year before the end of the war. Both boats have been modified with a schnorkel for running the diesel engines when submerged. The rigid air pipe, together with head valve to stop water running down into the boat, was housed under the deck casing. The duct bringing exhaust fumes up from the engine room can be seen on both boats and there is a clip for holding the schnorkel against the top of the conning tower.

Left: U43, a Type IXA, looking down on the conning tower from a partly extended periscope. The main hatch with an open lid can be seen by the men's feet. To the left is the stand for the torpedo aimer and to the right, behind Martin Becker, is the slot housing the circular radio direction finder aerial.

Right: This is the torpedo loading hatch of *U534*, showing how tight it was for a man to fit through. The hatches on the top of the pressure hull would normally not be opened once the boat put to sea because they were close to water level, so close that when the boat was trimmed for quick diving, waves could well be constantly washing over the top of them. This meant it would have been unlikely for the crew to open them unless specifically ordered to do so.

Right: U181, a long-range Type IXD2. Looking from the commander's control room inside the conning tower up through the open hatch. Hatches were basically all of a similar size and the larger boats did not have bigger entrances. Theoretically sea water washing into the conning tower should have closed the lid, but this was not to be relied upon and considerable volumes of water cascaded down before there was sufficient pressure to jam the rubber ring seal tight into its fitting. Usually the last man down would pull it shut and turn the locking wheel to prevent it from being blown open by depth charges.

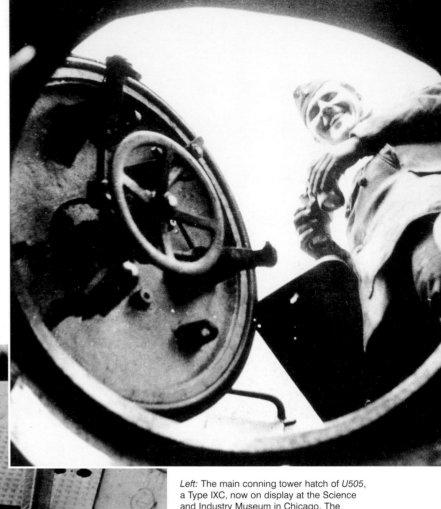

Left: The main conning tower hatch of *U505*, a Type IXC, now on display at the Science and Industry Museum in Chicago. The powerful spring counterbalanced the weight of the lid and usually allowed it to open slowly on its own. Very little effort was then required to pull it shut.

Right: The hatch inside the conning tower of *U505*, showing the locking mechanism.

Left: This man climbing out of the main conning tower hatch again demonstrates just how little room there was to fit through. Many things just could not be brought into the boat. Many radios, for example, had to be dismantled and reassembled on the inside.

Above: Looking forward in the central control room of *U995*, now on display by the Naval Memorial at Laboe near Kiel (Germany). The bottom of the shaft, leading up to the main hatch, can be seen in the top foreground. Behind it, with a cable running down, is the sky or navigation periscope. This head was usually not used during attacks because it was too conspicuous. The helmsman sat to the right of the circular doorway and the positions for the two hydroplane operators are on the other side of the L-shaped bench. The commander's cabin was on the far side of the circular hatch towards the left and the radio room was to the right. The chart table is just visible on the left.

Right: Looking up from the floor of the central control room while a man is blocking the hatch. Imagine this being a boarder climbing down into a boat still occupied. There was no way he could see what was going on below and he had to expose himself to a possible defender.

Right: Kptlt Günther Müller-Stöckheim, commander of *U67* (a Type IXC), giving some idea of size by standing next to the circular pressure-tight hatch leading forward from the central control room.

Left: U172 at play. This was a game whereby men raced from one end of the boat to the other and back again carrying a heavy block of ballast. Although such an undertaking might sound like torture, it was very much a requested activity to help pass the boring time of day. It was also a useful drill because during an alarm dive all the off duty men would rush forward, to help make the boat bow heavy, and everyone had to pass through this narrow hatch.

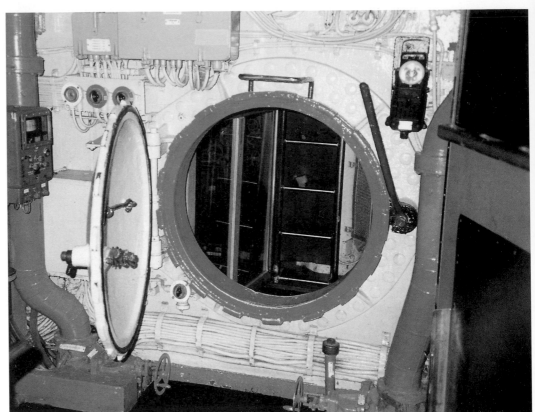

This page: Internal hatches in U-Bauer, a Type XXI, now on display at the Maritime Museum in Bremerhaven. Although a more modern boat than Types VII and IX, the hatches are very similar to those fitted to earlier boats of World War 2. Getting through them was indeed quite difficult, especially when carrying a tray full of hot food.

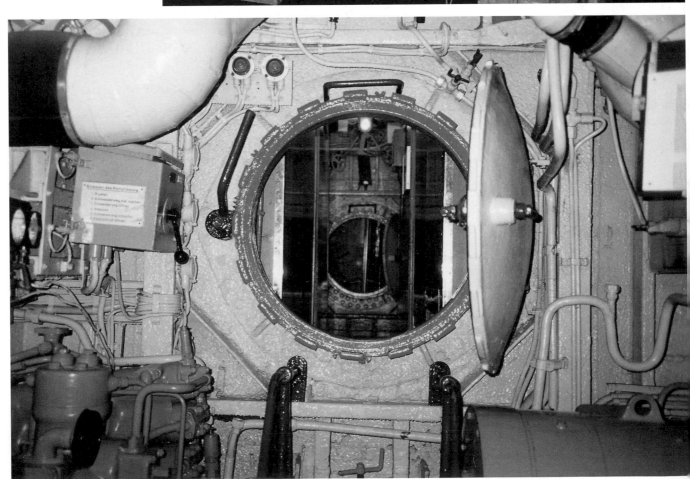

The **Nerve Centre** of a Type VII C.

1. Surface attack periscope. 2. Sky periscope. 3. Hohentwiel radar aerial. 4. Radar detection aerial. 5. Radio direction finder for long wave radio waves. 6. Hatch. 7. Commander's seat at periscope. 8. Pressurized cabin in conning tower. (Commander's position for submerged attacks.) 9. Periscope well. 10. Diving tank III. 11. Oil tank. 12. Battery room. 13. Water tap. 14. Circular pressurized door. 15. Control room. 16.

Commander's "cabin". 17. Galley (kitchen). 18. Lockers. 19. Bunks. 20. Pressurized walls. 21. Pressurized containers for ammunition. 22. Flag pole. 23. Upper gun platform. 24. Lower gun platform. 25. Light. 26. Magnetic compass. 27. Pressure hull wall. 28. Air duct to engine room. 29. Air intake. 30. Wave or spray deflector. 31. Wind deflector. 63. Accommodation. 64. Keel.

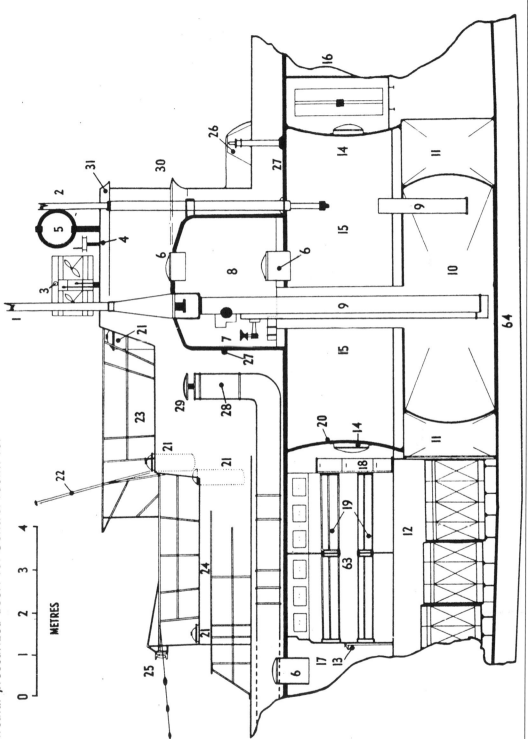

METRES

181

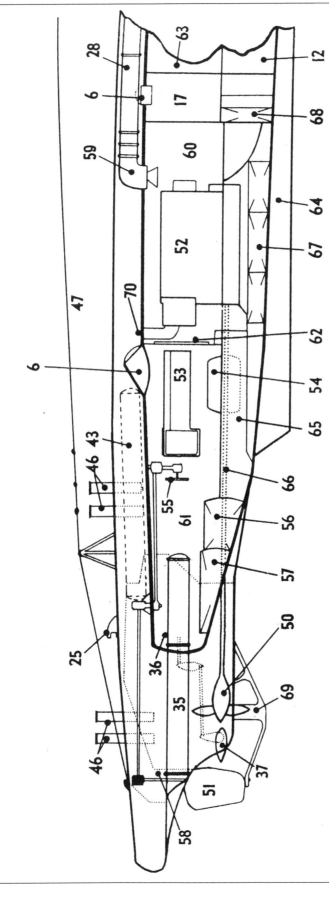

Section Through the Stern of a Type VII C

6. Hatch. 12. Battery room. 17. Galley (kitchen). 25. Light. 28. Air duct. 35. Torpedo tube. 36. Manual hydroplane control (only used in emergencies). 37. Hydroplane. 43. Storage space for torpedoes. 46. Bollard. 47. Jumping wire. 50. Propeller. 51. Rudder. 52. Diesel engine. 53. Control panel. 54. Electric motor. 55. Emergency steering wheel. 56. Torpedo tank. 57. Trim tank. 58. Position of diving tank I. 59. Air inlet into engine room. 60. Diesel engine room. 61. Rear torpedo and electro control room. 62. Door. 63. Accommodation. 64. Keel. 65. Storage space for torpedoes. 66. Propeller shaft (clutches not shown). 67. Various oil tanks. 68. Position of tanks for drinking water and used water tanks. 69. Propeller guard and bottom bracket for rudder. 70. Diesel exhaust.

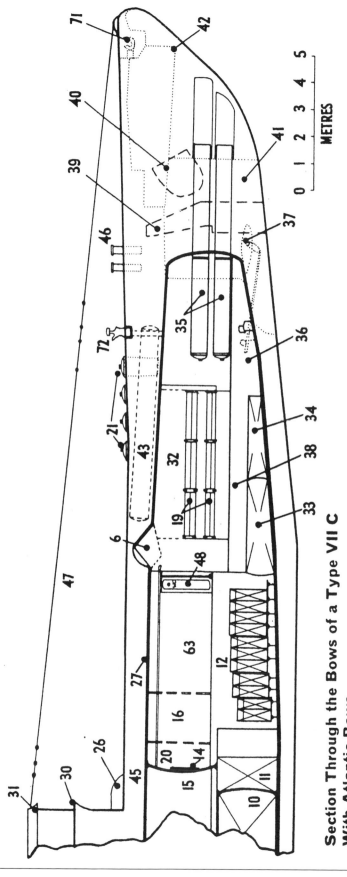

Section Through the Bows of a Type VII C With Atlantic Bows

6. Hatch. 10. Diving tank III. 11. Oil tank. 12. Battery room. 14. Circular pressurized door. 15. Control room. 16. Commander's "cabin". 19. Bunks. These could also be used for storing torpedoes. 20. Pressurized walls. 21. Pressurized containers for inflatable life rafts. 27. Pressure hull wall. 30. Wave or spray deflector. 31. Wind deflector. 32. Bow torpedo room with accommodation for crew. 33. Torpedo tank. 34. Trim tank. 35. Torpedo tube. 36. Manual hydroplane control (only used in emergencies). 37. Hydroplane. 38. Storage space for torpedoes. 39. Anchor chain locker. 40. Anchor hawse. 41. Position of diving tank II. 42. Stabilizing tank. 43. Storage space for torpedoes. 26. Magnetic compass. 45. Storage space for rigid schnorkel. 46. Bollard. 47. Jumping wire and aerial. (Prevents boat being caught in nets.) 48. Toilet. 63. Accommodation. 71. Hook and tow rope. 72. Winch.

Appendix III
Weather Trawlers

The study of weather ships is made more difficult by a number of confusing names and this, together with a shortage of German published records, has resulted in some ambiguous information having appeared. This problem of naming the boats is made more difficult because of a number of trawlers in different ports had identical names. The following is a complete list of all weather observation ships. Those marked with a star (*) were listed by Hinsley as having been of special interest to Bletchley Park.

Not all of the boats were used for weather observations throughout the entire war. Therefore some numbers have been used more than once.

WBS = *Wetterbeobachtungsschiff*
(Weather Observation Ship)

Adolf Vinnen	WBS 5
*August Wriedt**	WBS 1
Berlebek	WBS 7
Carl J. Busch	WBS3
*Coburg**	WBS 2
Externsteine	WBS 11
*Fritz Hohmann**	WBS 3
Gotland	WBS 10
Hermann	WBS 1 (ex-*Sachsen*)
Hessen	WBS 8
Hinrich Freese	WBS 4
*Lauenburg**	WBS 3 (also falsely listed in some books as Lauenberg)
Kehdingen	WBS 6
Merceditta	WBS 9
*München**	WBS 6
*Ostmark**	WBS 5 (there was also a Luftwaffe catapult ship with this name)
*Sachsen**	WBS 1 (later renamed Hermann)
*Sachsenwald**	WBS 7
Teutoburger Wald	WBS 12
Windhuk	WBS 10

Other relevant vessels were:

Krebs   Boarded during the Lofoten Raid.

V2623   Boarded in 1940. This also was a fishing boat which had been drawn into war service.

Locating records of these vessels in published sources is not easy and many of them did not even feature significantly in original Kriegsmarine documents. Since the boardings took place at times when the naval high command was faced with far more pressing problems than the loss of such small ships, this meant that they disappeared from the scene without the men in the naval high command being too deeply concerned about the incidents.

Finding photographs of the two weather ships captured as a result of suggestions from Bletchley Park has proved most difficult, but a few pictures of the *Sachsen* have been included to give some idea of their general appearance and enable the life aboard them to be visualised. For that reason, *Sachsen* has been added to the following table of technical data.

München
Builder	J. C. Tecklenborg, Wesermünde
Year built:	1927
Prewar home port:	Wesermünde
Gross registered tonnage:	306 tonnes
Maximum displacement:	680 tonnes
Length:	42.3m
Beam:	7.7m
Height:	3.5m
Engine:	Steam
Crew:	About 10

Lauenburg
Builder:	Schulte & Bruns, Emden
Year built:	1938
Prewar home port:	Bremen
Gross registered tonnage:	344 tonnes
Maximum displacement:	580 tonnes
Length:	41.5m
Beam:	7.7m
Height:	3.0m
Engine:	Diesel
Crew:	About 28

Sachsen
Builder:	Hugo Peters, Beidenfleth (Elbe)
Year built:	1938
Prewar home port:	Hamburg
Gross registered tonnage:	106 tonnes
Maximum displacement:	250 tonnes
Length:	23m
Beam:	6.3m
Height:	3.0m
Engine:	Diesel
Crew:	About 20

Appendix IV
Types of Convoy Escorts

The following table has been included to give some indication of the vital statistics of different escort types.

	Destroyer *Bulldog*	Sloop *Rochester*	Corvette *Aubrietia*	Frigate *Loch More*
Displacement	1360t	1105t	925t	1400t
Length	95m	76m	59m	94m
Beam	10m	10m	10m	12m
Height	4m	>3m	4.5m	5m
Speed	35kt	16kt	16kt	20kt
Complement	138	100	85	100
Completed	1931	1931	1940	1944

Appendix V
The Ireland Letter Code

The Kriegsmarine knew that some of its men would be captured in the event of war and therefore devised a secret letter code known as the Ireland code so they could communicate any useful information they might have in their letters home from prisoner of war camps. The code was made known only to commanders, senior officers and very few long-serving warrant officers. The next of kin, who were likely to receive such letters, were instructed to forward all mail from prison camps to the Supreme Naval Command. They were not aware of the code. Instead they had been told that experts might be able to draw some conclusions from the message.

The code worked quite simply by dividing the alphabet into three groups: letters A to I represented a dot in Morse code; letters J to R a dash and letters S to Z a gap. All that needed to be remembered were the letters I and R, the last in each set, hence the system became known as the Irland (Ireland) Code. The decisive letters were the first ones of any word, so it was just a case of composing the secret message in Morse code and then inventing some harmless text in which the words had the correct initial letters to match the coded sequence.

In addition to this there was another system for sending news of successes and the reasons for being sunk. Successes were reported by greetings at the end of the letter. For example: Versenkungen (sinkings) = viele Grüsse (many greetings or regards), Beschädigung (damage) = beste Grüsse (best regards), Schlachtschiff (battleship) = Schwester (sister), Kreuzer (cruiser) = Kind (child), Flugzeugträger (aircraft carrier) = Vetter (cousin), kein Erfolg (no success) = Nichte (niece — Nicht means no in German) and so on. Hence the message 'Schlachtschiff Hood wurde versenkt' could be written as 'Viele Grüsse an Schwester Hannah' ('Many greetings to sister Hannah').

Further Reading

Beesley, Patrick, *Very Special Intelligence*, Hamish Hamilton, London, 1977 and Doubleday, New York, 1978. (An interesting book dealing with Admiralty Intelligence by an officer who served there as Deputy Head of the Submarine Tracking Room.)

Bonatz, Heinz. *Seekrieg im Äther*, E. S. Mittler, Herford, 1981. (The author was Commander-in-Chief of the German Radio Monitoring Service.)

Busch, Rainer and Röll, Hans-Joachim, *Der U-Boot-Krieg 1939 bis 1945*. Vol 1, *Die deutschen U-Boot-Kommandanten*, Koehler/Mittler, Hamburg, Berlin, Bonn, 1996. Published in English by Greenhill as *U-boat Commanders*. (Brief biographies produced from the records of the German U-boot-Archiv. Sadly, the English edition has been published without the numerous corrections recorded by the Archive.)

— *Der U-Boot-Krieg 1939-1945*, E. S. Mittler & Sohn, Hamburg, Berlin and Bonn, 1999. (German U-boat losses from September 1939 to May 1945 from the records of the U-Boot-Archiv.)

Carter, Frank, *Codebreaking with the Colossus Computer*, The Bletchley Park Trust Reports, No 1, 1996.

— and Gallehawk, John, *The Enigma Machine and the Bombe*, The Bletchley Park Reports, No 9, 1998.

Compton-Hall, Richard, *The Underwater War 1939-45*, Blanford, Poole, 1982. (The author was the Director of the Royal Navy's Submarine Museum and this is by far the best book describing life in submarines.)

Connel, G. G., *Fighting Destroyer — The Story of HMS Petard*, William Kimber, London, 1976.

Dönitz, Karl, *Ten Years and 20 Days*, Weidenfeld & Nicolson, London, 1959.

Enever, Ted, *Britain's Best Kept Secret*, Sutton Publishing, Stroud, 1994 and 1999.

Gallehawk, John, *Naval Events and Enigma 1942-1943*, The Bletchley Park Reports, No 14, 1999.

— *How the Enigma Secret was Nearly Revealed*, The Bletchley Park Reports, No 11, 1998.

Giessler, Helmuth, *Der Marine-Nachrichten-und-Ortungsdienst*, J. F. Lehmanns, Munich, 1971.

Gröner, Erich, *Die deutschen Kriegsschiffe 1815-1945*, J. F. Lehmanns, Munich, 1968. (This is the standard book on the technical data of German warships. Much of the information is tabulated, making it relatively easy for non-German readers. However, the section dealing with U-boat losses contains a good proportion of questionable information.)

— *Die Handelsflotten der Welt, 1942*, J. F. Lehmanns, Munich, reprinted 1976. (Includes details of ships sunk up to 1942. This valuable publication was originally a confidential document and contains a complete list of ships, in similar style to Lloyd's *Register*. There is also a lengthy section with good line drawings.)

Harbon, John D., *The Longest Battle (The RCN in the Atlantic 1939-1945)*, Vanwell, Ontario, 1993.

Herzog, Bodo, *60 Jahre deutsche Uboote 1906-1966*, J. F. Lehmanns, Munich, 1968. (A useful book with much tabulated information.)

— *U-boats in Action*, Ian Allan, Shepperton and Podzun, Dorheim. (A pictorial book with captions in English.)

Hessler, Günter, and Hoschatt, et al, *The U-boat War in the Atlantic*, HMSO, 1989.

Hinsley, F. H., *British Intelligence in the Second World War*, HMSO, London, 1979.

— and Stripp, Alan, *Code Breaker*, Oxford University Press, Oxford, 1993.

Hirschfeld, Wolfgang, *Feindfahrten*, Neff, Vienna, 1982. (The secret diary of a U-boat radio operator compiled in the radio rooms of operational submarines. A most invaluable insight into the war and probably one of the most significant accounts of the war at sea.)

— *Das Letzte Boot — Atlantik Farewell*, Universitas, Munich, 1989. (The last journey of U234, surrender in the United States and life in prisoner of war camps.)

— and Geoffrey Brooks, *Hirschfeld — The Story of a U-boat NCO 1940-46*, Leo Cooper, London, 1996. (A fascinating English language edition of Hirschfeld's life in U-boats.)

Hodges, Andrew Alan, *Turing: The Enigma*, Burnet Books, London, 1983.

Högel, Georg, *Embleme Wappen Malings deutscher Uboote 1939-1945*, Koehlers, Hamburg, Berlin, Bonn, 1997. Published in English as *U-boat Emblems of World War II 1939-1945*, Schiffer Military History, Atglen, 1999. (An excellent work dealing with U-boat emblems, especially those which were painted on conning towers. Very well illustrated with drawings by the author who served in *U30* and *U110* during the war.)

Johnson, Brian, *The Secret War*, BBC, London, 1978.

Jung, D., Maass, M., and Wenzel, B., *Tanker und Versorger der deutschen Flotte 1900-1980*, Motorbuch, Stuttgart, 1981. (This excellent book is the standard reference work on the German supply system.)

Kahn, David, *Seizing the Enigma: The Race to Break the German U-boat codes, 1939-45*, Houghton Mifflin, Boston, 1991.

Kemp, Paul, *U-boats Destroyed*, Arms and Armour, London, 1997.

Kohnen, David, *Commanders Winn and Knowles: Winning the U-boat War with Intelligence 1939-1943*, The Enigma Press, Krakow, 1999. (An interesting book, although the name Rodger Winn is misspelled as Roger throughout.)

Lewin, Ronald, *Ultra goes to War*, Hutchinson, London, 1978.

Lohmann, W., and Hildebrand, H. H., *Die deutsche Kriegsmarine 1939-1945*, Podzun, Dorheim, 1956-1964. (This multi-volume work is the standard reference document on the German Navy, giving details of ships, organisation and personnel.)

Meister, Jürg, *Der Seekrieg in den osteuropäischen Gewässern 1941-1945*, J. F. Lehmanns, Munich, 1958. (Includes details of cruiser warfare in Arctic waters.)

Milner, Marc, *North Atlantic Run*, Naval Institute Press, Annapolis, 1985.

Möller, Eberhard, *Kurs Atlantik*, Motorbuch Verlag, Stuttgart, 1995.

Moore, Captain Arthur R., *A careless word ... a needless sinking*, American Merchant Marine Museum, Maine, 1983. (A detailed and well-illustrated account of ships lost during the war.)

Mulligan, Timothy P., *Neither Sharks Nor Wolves*, United States Naval Institute Press, Annapolis, 1999 and Chatham Publishing, London, 1999. (An excellent book about the men who manned the U-boats.)

Niestle, Axel, *German U-boat Losses during World War II*, Greenhill, London, 1998.

OKM (Supreme Naval Command), *Bekleidungs und Anzugsbestimmungen für die Kriegsmarine*, Berlin, 1935; reprinted Jak P. Mallmann Showell, 1979. (The official dress regulations of the German Navy.)

— *Rangliste der deutschen Kriegsmarine*, Mittler & Sohn, published annually, Berlin.

— *Handbuch für U-boot-Kommandanten*, Berlin, 1942

Pether, John, *The Post Office at War and Fenny Stratford Repeater Station*, The Bletchley Park Reports, No 12, 1998.

Preston, Anthony, *U-boats*, Arms and Armour Press, London, 1978. (Excellent photographs.)

Raeder, Erich, *Struggle for the Sea*, William Kimber, London, 1959.

— *My Life*, United States Naval Institute, 1960; translation of *Mein Leben*, F. Schlichtenmayer, Tübingen, 1956.

Rössler, Eberhard, *Die deutschen Uboote und ihre Werften*, Bernard & Graefe, Koblenz, 1979.

— *Geschichte des deutschen Ubootbaus*, Bernard & Graefe, Koblenz, 1986.

— *The U-boat*, Arms and Armour Press, London, 1981.

Rohwer, J., *Axis Submarine Successes of World War II 1939-45*, Greenhill, London, 1998.

— and Hümmelchen, G., *Chronology of the War at Sea 1939-1945*, Greenhill, London, 1992. (A good, solid and informative work. Well indexed and most useful for anyone studying the war at sea.)

— and Jäckel, Eberhard, *Die Funkaufklärung und ihre Rolle im 2. Weltkrieg*, Motorbuch Verlag, Stuttgart, 1979.

Roskill, Captain S. W., *The War at Sea*, HMSO, London, 1954, reprinted 1976. (Four volumes. The official history of the war at sea, 1939-45.)

— *The Secret Capture*, Collins, London, 1959.

Santoni, Alberto, *Ultra siegt im Mittelmeer*, Bernard & Graefe, Koblenz, 1985.

Sharpe, Peter, *U-boat Fact File*, Midland Publishing, Leicester, 1998.

Showell, Jak P. Mallmann, *The German Navy in World War Two*, Arms and Armour Press, London, 1979; Naval Institute Press, Annapolis, 1979 and translated as *Das Buch der deutschen Kriegsmarine*, Motorbuch Verlag, Stuttgart, 1982. (Covers history, organisation, the ships, code-writers, naval charts and a section on ranks, uniforms, awards and insignias by Gordon Williamson. Named by the United States Naval Institute as 'One of the Outstanding Naval Books of the Year'.)

— *U-boats under the Swastika*, Ian Allan, Shepperton, 1973; Arco, New York, 1973 and translated as *Uboote gegen England*, Motorbuch, Stuttgart, 1974. (A well-illustrated introduction to the German U-boat Arm, which is now one of the longest-selling naval books in Germany.)

— *U-boats under the Swastika*, Ian Allan, Shepperton, 1987; Naval Institute Press, Annapolis, 1987. (A second edition with different photos and new text of the above title.)

— *U-boat Command and the Battle of the Atlantic*, Conway Maritime Press, London, 1989; Vanwell, New York, 1989. (A detailed history based on the U-boat Command's war diary.)

— *Germania International*, Journal of the German Navy Study Group. Now out of print.

— *U-boat Commanders and their Crews*, The Crowood Press, Marlborough, 1998.

— *German Navy Handbook 1939-1945*, Sutton Publishing, Stroud, 1999.

— *U-boats in Camera 1939-1945*, Sutton Publishing, Stroud, 1999.

U-Boot-Archiv, *Das Archiv* (German), *The U-boat Archive* (English language). (A journal published twice a year for members of FTU, U-Boot-Archiv, D-27478 Cuxhaven-Altenbruch. Please enclose two International Postal Reply Coupons if asking for details.)

Verband Deutscher Ubootsfahrer, *Schaltung Küste*. (Journal of the German Submariners' Association.)

Wagner, Gerhard (Ed), *Lagevorträge des Oberbefehlshabers der Kriegsmarine vor Hitler*, J. F. Lehmanns, Munich, 1972. Translated as *Fuehrer Conferences on Naval Affairs*, Greenhill, London, reprinted with new introduction 1990. (Originally the English language edition was published before the German version.)

Welchman, Gordon, *The Hut Six Story*, M. M. Baldwin, Cleobury Mortimer, Shropshire, 1997.

Wescombe, Peter, and Gallehawk, John, *Getting back into SHARK*, The Bletchley Park Trust Reports, No 5, 1997.

West, Nigel, *GCHQ The Secret Wireless War 1900-86*, Weidenfeld and Nicolson, London, 1986.

Williamson, Gordon and Pavlovik, Darko, *U-boat Crews 1914-45*, Osprey, London, 1995. (A most interesting book with excellent colour drawings and black and white photographs.)

Winterbotham, F. W., *The Ultra Secret*, Weidenfeld and Nicolson, London, 1974. (The author was Chief of the Air Department of the Secret Intelligence Service during the war and was responsible for the organisation, distribution and security of Ultra.)

Winton, John, *Ultra at Sea*, Leo Cooper, London, 1988. (About breaking the U-boat radio codes.)

Witthöft, Hans Jürgen, *Lexikon zur deutschen Marinegeschichte*, Koehler, Herford, 1977. (An excellent two-volume encyclopaedia.)

Wynn, Kenneth, *U-boat Operations of the Second World War*, Chatham, London, 1997.

Index